RETURN OF THE CHILDREN OF LIGHT

RETURN OF THE CHILDREN OF LIGHT

Incan and Mayan Prophecies for a New World

Judith Bluestone Polich

Bear & Company
Rochester, Vermont

Bear & Company
One Park Street
Rochester, Vermont 05767
www.InnerTraditions.com

Library of Congress Cataloging-in-Publication Data

Polich, Judith Bluestone, 1948-
    Return of the children of light : Incan and Mayan prophecies for a new world
/ Judith Bluestone Polich
        p. cm.
    Originally published: Santa Fe, NM : Linkage Pub., 1999.
    Includes bibliographical references and index.
    ISBN 978-1-879181-69-4
        1. Incas—Religion—Miscellanea. 2.Prophecies (Occultism)—Peru. 3.
Mayas—Religion—Miscellanea. 4. Prophecies (Occultism)—Mexico. 5. Spiritual
Life—Miscellanea. I. Title.

    BF1812.P4 P65 2001
    299'.784152—dc21

2001046111

Printed and bound in the United States by Lake Book Manufacturing, Inc.

10 9 8 7

Text design and layout by Kathleen Sparkes

DEDICATION

This book is dedicated to the god-like beings of our mythological past who came from the future to show us who we might become.

ACKNOWLEDGMENTS

I am grateful to the many people who encouraged, inspired, and guided me in the process of writing and producing *Return of the Children of Light*. I would in particular like to thank Ellen Kleiner and her staff at Blessingway Author Services, and John Lyons-Gould at Piñon Publications for their editorial assistance, as well as David Christian Hamblin of Blessingway Books for his guidance.

I am very thankful for the sustaining nourishment provided at critical junctures by my dear friends Mara Senese, Trigve Despues, and Ruth Rusca. I am blessed with a partner, Gayle Dawn Price, to whom I owe a special gratitude for her editorial assistance and her support in innumerable ways through the breadth and depth of this journey. And finally my eternal gratitude to all those who helped light my path, including don Miguel Ruiz, H. H. the Dalai Lama, Sai Baba, and Mark Griffin.

CONTENTS ✿

PREFACE

My first mystical experience occurred 20 years ago. I was 32 years old and had lived in Wisconsin all my life. I had just finished law school at the University of Wisconsin in Madison and was driving cross-country to Boston with all my possessions piled in my old Toyota. Having left my home, my marriage of seven years, and my family, I was beginning a new life. Soon after crossing the Canadian–United States border into Maine, I became entranced by a small blue mountain in the distance. I drove toward it, as if magnetically drawn there by a force I couldn't understand.

Two hours before sunset, I arrived at the base of Mt. Blue, where I grabbed a blanket and started to ascend. The climb took me along a tumbling mountain stream; through dense, colorful thickets of fall foliage; and up above the treeline, where blueberry bushes bunched up amid lichen-covered granite. When I reached the top, I discovered I had the sparse summit, including a breathtaking and welcoming small glacier lake, to myself. As the sun set, I meditated and then spent the night listening to the mountain's secrets.

At dawn I sat by the lake's edge, my attention deep within myself. Suddenly, as the sun rose, my entire being was flooded—first with wave after wave of brilliant white light, then with wave after wave of iridescent rainbow light. It was as if I had been awakened and engendered by the light, for the pulsing energy that surged through me was unlike anything I had ever experienced. It filled me with deep love, a sense of well-being, and a penetrating clarity.

Several hours later, when I began to walk down the mountain to reenter the world, I realized that everything had subtly yet decisively changed. The light of the world had taken on a new brilliance, making all of nature vividly alive. My awareness of the surroundings was more immediate and empathic, and I felt interconnected with the energies of everything around me. In some respects I am still coming down from that mountain.

Since this dazzling encounter with the light two decades ago, I have had numerous transcendent experiences, many of which occurred in spectacular natural settings and ancient ruins. The experiences were all light-filled and imbued with messages. Slowly, I have come to understand my experiences and to comprehend some of the reasons why our world's sacred sites hold so much power.

Before gaining insight into these events, I—like any sane and reasonable person—tended to discount them. I was, after all, a lawyer with a well-trained rational mind. At the same time, I knew my experiences were not drug-induced hallucinations or imaginative flights of fantasy, but rather encounters with real forces. I couldn't understand them, so I simply compartmentalized. I told myself they were experiences in nonordinary realities (those not perceivable with the five senses) and left it at that. Only years later did I realize they were part of an ancient legacy. Slowly, the child of light, the god-seed hidden within me, began to awaken.

According to the cultural perspective I grew up with, if God was not dead, then he was at least far removed from my reality. In line with the scientific objectivity of the time, I was taught that if something were true, it could be perceived with the five senses and externally measured. I learned that only a layer or two of my neocortex separated me from other animals and that evolution was a fact, not a theory. From the standpoint of my Judeo-Christian tradition and of Western mythology, the human condition was depressing. Banished from paradise and tainted with original sin, humankind's only opportunity for redemption existed in some force outside itself.

By contrast, my experiences in other dimensions gradually gave me an altogether different perspective on the human condition. Each new lucid experience presented a piece of the puzzle until finally, during a trip to the ancient sites of the Peruvian Andes, a more complete vision of our collective human condition took shape. But before I could truly assimilate this vision, I had to pursue many avenues of exploration. I visited sacred sites in Europe and the British Isles—from Delphi to Stonehenge—and, like so many others entering these ancient energy fields, I felt something palpable yet undefinable. I even took up dowsing (the practice of detecting energy fields, especially those associated with water flowing underground) to refine my ability to perceive such energy. But, early on, I could not fully comprehend the relationships between various phenomena I was experiencing.

Then, in the mid-1980s, I discovered the ancient sites of the Americas. On a trip with a cultural anthropologist to learn about shamanism on the Yucatán peninsula (land of the Maya), an extraordinary experience radically altered my perception. One afternoon a few of us went to a recently discovered cave that had been used by the ancient Maya for ceremonial purposes. We entered a large, dark chamber filled with the strong smell of copal (a resin from tropical trees that was often burned in ancient ceremonial practice). As my eyes adjusted, I saw a spectacular sight. In the center of the chamber was a stalagmite tree with branches that touched the cave's ceiling—a representation of the tree of life. What an amazing inspiration this image must have been to the ancients. Rooted in the underworld, the tree stretched up to the heavens, as if bridging the two worlds. Around the tree were copal burners and other ceremonial objects that I was told had lain there untouched for hundreds of years. The energy was almost intoxicating.

As we crawled through a narrow passageway to an underground stream, I lost consciousness and entered a dream state in which I experienced an initiation. Amid drumbeats and wafts of burning copal, I was the initiate, a young warrior. My muscles were firm and taut; my dark, finely chiseled features, distinctively Mayan. My face was painted in vivid colors, and brilliant iridescent feathers framed my head. As I lay there in the darkness, I suddenly saw above me the sinister face of a jaguar—the mask of the great priest. I took what I was sure would be my last breath and surrendered myself, holding my focus steadily on my inner light, as I had been taught to do. As a knife descended into my body, I felt no pain but instead gave my heart fully and freely to the light, enabling my consciousness to ascend and merge with the ageless force within the light. As quickly as I had entered the dream state, I reemerged to normal reality. Gasping for breath, I regained awareness of my immediate reality on the floor of the cave. Momentarily disoriented, I did not know who or where I was. Then

I heard a man talking about fish that lived in the underground stream; they were blind, he said, because their forebears had undergone a mutation, never having seen the light. I continued crawling to the stream, where I spent a long time drinking from the cool, sweet water.

For days afterward I was shaken by this experience, which had been so vivid that it seemed more real than life. Then it faded into just another dream as I went back to my office and filled my mind with the mundane tasks of filing divorces, researching real estate titles, and drafting wills. In time I almost forgot about my afternoon in the cave.

A few years later I met don Miguel Ruiz, a *nagual* (Mesoamerican shaman) who traced his lineage to ancient Toltecs. *Nagual* practices, which are still observed in indigenous cultures throughout Mesoamerica, rely on the mastery of nonordinary realities. I was familiar with the term "*nagual*" from the writings of Carlos Castaneda, an anthropology professor who had apprenticed with a Yaqui indian shaman of *nagual* descent.

Don Miguel Ruiz appeared nothing like my grand conception of a *nagual*, who I had imagined as otherworldly and unaffected by the enroachment of modern culture. This *nagual* was a little brown Mexican man in his thirties, dressed up as an L. A. dude. He wore spiffy, open-collar shirts with gaudy, gold necklaces; sang Beatles songs in broken, almost incomprehensible English; and told everyone who came to his lectures seeking wisdom to simply "be happy." Nonetheless, working with him over the next six years proved pivotal to my spiritual growth. Among other things, he opened doorways to other dimensions at Teotihuacán, the famous pyramids near Mexico City, and he taught me about unconditional love.

On my first trip to Teotihuacán, I was on top of the Pyramid of the Sun with don Miguel, another young *nagual,* and a visitor from the United States. Don Miguel and the young *nagual* were performing some kind of ritual, but I had no idea what they were doing. Then I saw to my astonishment that their hands were made of millions of stars, swirling galaxies of light, the very matrix of the universe. I quickly looked away in disbelief, thinking that what I had seen could not possibly be true. Yet when I looked back, I saw the same vision.

After leaving the pyramid, the four of us stayed awake late into the night talking about our experiences at the ruins. Don Miguel had put me through specific training exercises all day, practices designed to help me loosen my grip on ordinary reality and encourage nonordinary perception. Prodding me into the unfamiliar, he had deliberately provoked me numerous times, challenging the way I thought about things and making me feel foolish and uncomfortable. And I was angry at how he kept pushing my buttons with behaviors that seemed utterly inane.

Tired and immersed in inner turmoil, I looked at don Miguel as he sat beside me and saw nothing but unconditional love. At that moment I realized he would love me unequivocally as I struggled to break free of my illusions. And although for months afterward my mind periodically convinced me of the impossibility of seeing hands as swirling galaxies of light, I now know that I saw the *naguals* as they truly are, and that I too am made of swirling galaxies of light. I continued to fight this revelation with all the resistance my rational mind could muster until truth eventually proved more powerful than reason.

After this first trip to Teotihuacán, the foundations of my world began to unravel. A long-term relationship fell apart, and life seemed meaningless. For years I underwent radical shifts in perception and emotional disequilibrium. Following transcendental experiences I would plummet into despair. It took me some time to understand that the encounters I was having with bright fields of light were simultaneously revealing my own hidden darkness. Subsequently integrating this understanding into my perception of everyday reality proved even more challenging.

Eventually, I learned that the *nagual* belief system contains tools to help with such integration. One of these is stalking. Stalking, as the term implies, is the process of pursuing prey. According to the *nagual* tradition, our greatest prey is our mind—especially our limited beliefs and our unconscious aspects of Self. We stalk in order to bring these elements to consciousness, to enhance self-awareness. Many workshops and books describe stalking techniques; those I used involved examining my emotions and thought patterns, learning to trace them to their sources, and eliminating those that no longer served me—thereby reclaiming the energy I had lost through ineffective behaviors.

After one of my early plummets into despair, I decided I would travel to India to experience the energy of the great masters, the closest contemporary equivalent we may have to the ancient idea of a god-man (a divine being in human form). One winter day, after a 24-hour bus trip from New Delhi, I arrived in Dharamsala, the center of the Tibetan government exiled in a beautiful mountainous region at the base of the Himalayas. There, by incredible good fortune, I was able to arrange an audience with H. H. the Dalai Lama. On the afternoon of the audience, the courtyard of the monastery where he resides was filled with visitors and red-robed monks. We waited silently (with increasing expectation) for what seemed like hours. Suddenly, after a burst of colorful regalia, H. H. the Dalai Lama appeared. Despite the external pomp and circumstance, he walked shyly and humbly among us, as if genuinely wondering what all the fuss was about. He then began to bestow blessings. When he blessed me, I felt an immediate transmission of energy and an unimaginable state of mental clarity.

My experiences in India convinced me that god-men are not only mythic beings but also humans who demonstrate a high level of spiritual functioning and have extraordinary capabilities. Such beings show us, as latent god-seeds, what our true potential is. It is my belief that the seemingly remarkable abilities of god-men are innate potentials in all of us and will be more widely accessible to humankind in the near future.

In southern India, near Bangalore, I stood within the energy field of the luminous god-man known as Sai Baba, whose radiant aura can be seen from blocks away. I could not only see his enormous energy field, but for months afterward I felt pierced by his penetrating love. Farther south I visited one of India's most famous pilgrimage sites—the sacred mountain Arunacula. All around the base of the mountain are caves where saints and holy men known as *sadhus* live and meditate for decades at a time. Entering one of these caves is like stepping into a crystal programmed at high frequency. My awareness shifted, my mind became very still, and my perceptions intensified.

As a result of my travels in Hindu and Buddhist countries, and in the shamanic cultures of the Americas, and my years of experiencing nonordinary realities, I have come to understand that the reality I routinely perceive and interact in is only a dream—a culturally formed and communicated worldview we all agree on. The tangible aspects of this consensual view are rooted in a world of three dimensions and linear time, resulting in a space-time perception that is predictable, measurable, and objective. Beyond this space/time continuum are other realities. The microworld of quantum physics, the macroworld of galactic interactions, the dreamtime of Australian Aborigines, and many mystical states all seem to defy the laws of Newtonian physics.

I have come to realize that *all* humans have the ability to function within multiple realities. Like the legendary god-men, we are multidimensional beings who can learn not only to perceive multiple, simultaneous realities but also to function in the higher worlds these perceptions open us to.

I have been to Teotihuacán many times since my initial visit with don Miguel Ruiz. It was there—a site known as "the place where man become God"—that I awakened several years ago into what I call "the angel light." I was sitting on top of the Pyramid of the Moon, watching the crowd pass from the citadel to the pyramids along the Avenue of the Dead. The light that day was clear and highly refined. Suddenly, the light began to communicate with me in the form of images and words traveling in wavelike patterns. With each wave came a heightened awareness that gave me information and altered my worldview. I ceased to exist as a separate entity and instead knew I was part of an unbroken wholeness. I began to merge with the angel light, consciously surrendering to the lucidity that overtook me. While I was at all times conscious of sitting on top of the pyramid, I could also feel myself extending beyond the confines of my body. The light with which I merged interpenetrated my body, but I was not my body. I had become one with the collective force of cosmic light—a wave of galactic information in the form of pure light—which, as an act of pure love, interpenetrates this planet.

Moreover, during this experience I realized that this wave of light is all I have ever been and that everything else is an illusion. I saw things as they are from the viewpoint of the light that engenders all consciousness. I understood that I am merely a projection—a thought form, an aspect of a collective force of light that is by choice encased in matter.

In this state of heightened awareness, I sensed the inevitability of light prevailing upon this planet. I also perceived a higher order unfolding from what may be a cosmic hologram, comprehending that all matter will be uplifted to levels of consciousness as yet undreamed of. I witnessed waves and waves of the gentle conquering force of cosmic light descend and enter form, transforming our world forever. I saw primordial reality as it exists in an unbroken wholeness that carries intent and knew that I was merely a reflection of this higher intent. In short, I now saw the world through new eyes—the way the angelic realms, and the higher forces they represent, see us. And I knew that deep within my being, in the very structure of my DNA, something long hidden had awakened. I was sprouting.

The lucidity I experienced on the Pyramid of the Moon marked a profound turning point in my life. My worldview and my perception of myself dramatically and inalterably shifted. Having realized I was part of a larger consciousness, I began to open to new levels of my inherent multidimensionality.

Later that year, I had the opportunity to visit Machu Picchu, the magnificent temple-citadel of the ancient Inca people, 50 miles northwest of Cuzco, Peru. At the time, I knew nothing about the Inca or their prophecies. Either by fate or by coincidence, I arrived at Machu Picchu at a most interesting time. Forest fires had recently ravaged the surrounding mountains and had miraculously stopped at the base of the ruins. The fires had brought not only a physical cleansing to the landscape, but a great spiritual cleansing, and apparently much more. A *pag'o* (shaman), told us that since the cleansing of the sacred mountains that surround Machu Picchu, several ancient gateways to energy fields had recently opened.

To the early Inca, as well as to many indigenous people worldwide, gateways were far more than a metaphor; they were a *living reality*, and their presence was felt in many dimensions at once. The Inca believed they descended from divine light, serving as its divine emissaries in physical form. By about A.D. 1525, the Inca had determined that their access to higher worlds of more refined frequencies, or light fields, was diminishing. Possibly they understood that frequencies of matter were slowing down, and the pull of an increasingly dense material world was limiting their access to higher worlds. They referred to this change as the closing of the gateways. Interestingly, these gateways were not only celestial portals but also entryways to individual higher consciousness.

After much personal experience and investigation of historical events, I have come to believe that due to the convergence of various earthly and galactic circumstances, the gateways for traversing dimensions are again opening. A new order, inviting increased human potential, is beginning to unfold.

During an evening at Machu Picchu, under a sky filled with brilliant stars, I stepped through one of the ancient gateways, discovering that, as pure light, I was eternal and without limits. In this state of lucidity, I understood that I was not separate from the rest of creation, that such separation truly is illusion, and that I am merely a unique expression of a dynamic whole. This was not new information, but because I perceived it energetically, I comprehended it with a depth my mind alone could never have grasped.

On my last day in Peru, I went to an ancient site called the Muru Doorway in the Lake Titicaca region near the Bolivian border, an area credited as being the origin of the mythical children of light. On the way there our native guide, Jorge, told us the story of the legendary Amanumuru—a great god-man who one day walked through a gateway known as the Muru Doorway and returned to his celestial home. The story triggered deep emotions in me, causing me to cry out of a desire to go home, too. For decades after my initial experiences in higher dimensions, my reentry into ordinary reality was often difficult. At times I was worldweary, all too aware of the harshness and cruelty of human circumstances. Although I understood in some vague way that I was a multidimensional being, I felt that an aspect of my light came from far outside this planetary system. I longed to merge with the source of consciousness itself. Clearly, I had not yet grounded my multidimensionality.

The Muru Doorway is a rectangular indentation carved into a large vertical plate of rock with a small circular indentation at its center. As you stand in this doorway, your navel lines up with the center circle, which looks out at Lake Titicaca and aligns directly with the Island of the Sun (an island in the middle of the lake thought to be the source of all life). Although the red rock landscape of the area is similar to the spectacular rock outcroppings found around my present home in northern New Mexico, I have never experienced a landscape of such mythic power as I witnessed that day near Lake Titicaca.

Surrounding me were natural sculptures that symbolically portrayed the transformation of the human seed. First, we climbed a 100-foot-wide undulating rock surface that resembled the body of a snake, representing the first level of Andean reality: the underworld. Next, we slid down rocks shaped like the back of a puma, signifying the second level of Andean reality: the world of manifestation. We then entered a small valley where a natural stone formation depicted a giant caterpillar awaiting metamorphosis. High in the cliffs on the other side of the valley was a spectacular rock shaped like a butterfly ascending into the azure sky.

The otherworldly energy field around the Muru Doorway induces trance states. As I stood in the doorway, I extended my arms straight out to the sides and placed my womb against the center circle. Standing there in the shape of a cross, I began to see brilliant glyphs and images. These I took to be a glimpse at how we are perceived by the great Elohim—the god-men of the mythic past, the great angels of the Judeo-Christian tradition who brought spiritual consciousness into form. I saw the beautiful seedbeds that represent the evolving consciousness of humanity. I perceived the great love and benevolence with which god-men attend their garden and how they irradiate the clusters of luminous god-seeds that make up humanity with the purest divine light. I witnessed how they have nourished our growth for an almost immeasurable time, and the great joy they feel when a seed finally sprouts.

After years of stumbling blindly in the darkness, I slowly found my bearings in this more lucid realm of human multidimensionality. To integrate my new awareness, I had to let go of ingrained false beliefs about my world and myself. Over time I came to understand that a new chapter of the human story is unfolding—a segment of which is expressed in the mythologies of ancient peoples around the planet.

As was predicted in ancient texts and prophecies, nonindigenous cultures are now beginning to perceive what ancient cultures accepted. Pioneers in science and in the study of human consciousness are enhancing our understanding of human potential. New findings in quantum physics and cosmology are expanding our comprehension of human capabilities and of the universe itself.

There is indeed something new under the sun—a different dynamic unfolding in the human story. A higher order is beginning to reshape both our world perspective and our view of ourselves. As the ancients predicted, *the human god-seed is beginning to awaken.*

INTRODUCTION

WE LIVE IN A TIME DESCRIBED BY RENOWNED MYTHOLOGIST Joseph Campbell as a "terminal moraine of myths and mythic symbols." We have only fragments left of the rituals and symbols that once gave meaning to human existence. The old stories we tell about ourselves no longer inspire or enliven because they are disconnected from a whole system of belief and practice. In short, the old gods are dead. On the bright side, however, new ones are beginning to emerge.

Glimpses of the forms these new gods will take can be found in many early mythologies, including those originating in Egypt, Africa, Tibet, and other parts of Asia; among the Hopi Indians of the United States; and in other portions of the Americas. These cultural myths, unlike modern religious doctrines, do not lay claim to "the truth" for all people of all times. On the contrary, indications are that early cultures knew that each held a *piece* of the truth, the whole of which may be woven together from a multitude of different strands. It has also been suggested that ideas germinating simultaneously in diverse places eventually cross-pollinate, enriching the whole of humanity. For now, as the pollen-laden breezes continue to blow, only one thing remains certain: *all world mythologies mirror the divine.*

This book presents a glimpse of human existence as seen through the lens of the early people inhabiting Mesoamerica and Peru, particularly the Maya and Inca—a lens that will serve as a useful portal for viewing the coming New Age. Why Mesoamerica and Peru? In part, because the myths and prophecies of these enigmatic ancient cultures are rarely or erroneously addressed and deserve greater exposure. And more importantly, because their perspectives appear to play a formative role in today's unfolding human consciousness.

Certainly, the idea of a human god-seed is hardly unique to the Maya and Inca. Many early cultures saw themselves as children of light. What *is* unique about their fecund idea of divinely engendered human beings is the eclectic revisioning of the human dream it is spawning. Research emerging from such diverse realms as quantum physics, cosmology, holography, and the study of human consciousness suggests that we are in the midst of a massive restructuring, altering both our perception of reality and our role in shaping it.

This new view of reality informs us that we are part of a larger whole; that we exist as fields within fields of increasingly refined energies; that ultimately we are beings of light, seeds of a tree of divine consciousness that fills the entire cosmos. Similarly, Mayan and Incan myths tell us that long ago, divine consciousness was seeded on this third planet from the sun creating the prodigy of an ancient divine lineage. Synthesizing the old understandings with the new findings, we learn that the codes to awakening our ancestral endowment—namely, our inner light—may lie hidden within the structure of our DNA. One by one, as we begin to remember who we are, a new consciousness will emerge. Then as soon as this revisioning reaches a critical mass, it will trigger an evolutionary leap to a new human species—the long-awaited, quantumly endowed spiritual human known to ancient cultures as the child of light. Throughout this book, I refer to this new human as the god-seed.

Where are we now in this unfolding adventure? We are entering an era marked by a new millennium, a new world-age, and a new precessional period. Replacing the fading worldview of unchanging, three-dimensional space within continuous time is a revolutionary worldview that tells us we exist in a dynamic state of "unbroken wholeness." In other words, as you will see in the pages that follow, we are well on our way to a collective transformation.

Although this book contains substantial documentation, I am not a scholar. My purpose has been simply to synthesize information from a variety of sources. As such, the book is best approached as a narrative tapestry infused with fact, oral transmission, and human imagination.

To understand the story of the human god-seed—an archetype, or blueprint, for the development of human consciousness—we must first step through some conceptual doorways. In Chapter 1 we'll be leaving behind the flash and glamour of our materialistic society and immersing ourselves in a world alive with shamanic activity. This chapter tells the story of the god-seed from the perspective of a young Inca priestess named Wayu—a *mamacona*, or Virgin of the Sun (women disciples of the ancient arts who served the *pachamama*, or Cosmic Mother)—who lived about 500 years ago in the high citadel of the Peruvian Andes we now call Machu Picchu. The information that inspires Wayu's story is drawn from both mythological and historical sources; it is best read, not so much for detail, as for an overall sense of perspective.

As you will quickly discover, Wayu's world was multi-dimensional. She perceived all matter as conscious and could see energy within forms. These faculties, together with her capacity to function in several realities at once, sprung forth as a result of her training. Most importantly, she understood that she was a god-seed, a child of light. Having tapped into the spiritually enlivened worldview of her ancestors, she managed to sustain herself in the years approaching A.D. 1525—an era of crisis in the Inca empire, a time of *pachacuti* or rapid change. The Incan word *pacha* means both "the world" and "time," whereas *cuti* is defined as "to overturn." And indeed, Wayu's world, much like our own, was about to be radically transformed.

Chapter 1 will immerse you in mythology, and I hope it will cause a corresponding shift in your overall worldview. Chapter 2 looks at who the Inca and Maya really were. With the help of new disciplines like archeoastronomy, this chapter dispels common stereotypes and misunderstandings about these ancient cultures and focuses on aspects of their teachings that create a new and powerful version of the human creation story.

Chapter 3 is the longest and, in some ways, the most pivotal chapter of the book. It gives the reader an in-depth understanding of concepts like world-ages and sacred correspondence that are critical to comprehending correlations to the emergence of new-sciences and the spiritual applications found later in the book. Take your time, have patience, and read with the understanding that what you are learning will eventually enable you to access modern applications of ancient wisdom.

In contrast to the current "hype" and anxiety surrounding the coming of the new millennium, the ancient mystical teachings of the high Andes are positive, practical teachings based on an understanding of human beings as engendered beings of light. Chapter 4 examines these Andean prophecies for the New Age, a new world-age that is now dawning and cycles of time much larger and significant than anything our modern culture has known.

Chapter 5 brings the discoveries of quantum physics and other new sciences into focus, in light of the ancient teachings. We are entering an age that offers the potential for great transformation of the human consciousness, and we need to understand what it means to awaken into true quantum beings—to function in a nonordinary reality that is our individual and collective birthright. Chapter 6 highlights sacred sites worldwide as tools for transformation, focusing on how they were intended to be used and how they ground our experience in the powerful context of myth.

Finally, we have an opportunity in this coming New Age to reenvision ourselves as a human species. In Chapter 7, I hope you will see that *who* we are and *what* we are meant to accomplish is more exciting than anything you have ever considered.

THE MYTH OF SEED

The seeds went forth through myriads of time,
Penetrating layered universes
Until they found their way to fertile sands
At the water's edge.

There they took root
Beneath a harsh sun
And waited through the dark and violent night
Until, kissed by a new spring light they awoke.

A seed awoke,
and drawing from deep within its hidden past,
The seed brought forth new life.
The light of its essence took form.

From pure potential, form sprang into being.
Where barrenness had been, there was life.
And as the god-seeds awakened one by one
The earth sang out her delight.

And so it came to pass,

That this world was transformed.
And the seeds set their many progeny adrift—
God-seeds in search of fertile ground
God-seeds of a new frequency of light.

1

KEEPERS
OF THE SEED

Wᴀʏᴜ ʜᴀᴅ ᴏᴠᴇʀsʟᴇᴘᴛ. Tʜᴇ sᴜɴ ᴡᴏᴜʟᴅ sᴏᴏɴ ʀɪsᴇ. She quickly grabbed her turquoise tunic, arranged her long, dark tasseled hair into place, and hurried to join the others in the courtyard. There, only the embers of the fire remained, and the morning air was still cool. She wished she had taken the warm alpaca blanket she had left behind in her haste. Already the Old One was deep in prayer. Wayu took her position prostrate in the direction of the first ray of light, which was the purest light, hoping their prayers to the Creator, Wiraccocha, would be heard.

The Old One began:

> *Wiraccocha*
> > *Hear our prayers.*
> > *We cry out to you.*
> > *Our hearts are one heart.*
> > *Do not abandon us.*
> *Wiraccocha*
> > *We are your children,*
> > *Your children of light.*
> > *We surrender to your will.*

As the light penetrated the citadel known to outsiders as Machu Picchu, located in the remote high plateau above the sacred valley, the mountains awoke and took shape, radiating layers of vivid emerald green and stretching upward, embracing a hazy azure sky. First Machu Picchu then Wayna Picchu and the other sacred mountains revealed themselves. While the first rays danced on the mountaintops, the crimson aura of Father Sun rose above the sun gate. Raising her head from prayer, Wayu was transfixed by the loving radiance of the sun burning through the doorway of the old mountain. The light pierced her heart with its purity as Father Sun answered, blessing her with his love.

She stood now with the others, facing Father Sun's ascent, listening intently to inner rhythms. What was it she had seen in her dream? She was with her Lightgiver, her teacher and caregiver. They were at the sacred river, down below at the jungle's edge. She turned and found her Lightgiver staring at her. But now she was not sure of the meaning of the dream. She would discuss it with her Lightgiver later.

The morning ritual was soon complete. Like the other initiates, Wayu had no time to linger after Father Sun awakened. She hurried to complete her chores and prepare herself for the day's lessons. First, she had to fetch water from the heart of the water spirit. As she walked briskly, she moved with a grace well beyond her years, her delicate frame barely touching the worn pathway. Though still a child, she was tall and willowy. Her finely chiseled features bore the characteristics of the royal lineage (Inca): high cheekbones, ebony-colored hair, penetrating dark eyes, and a pronounced willful brow. Yet something set her apart. She radiated an uncommon aura of otherworldliness.

As Wayu passed the first terrace, she paused briefly, giving thanks to the water spirit for the life that water provided. Soon it would be planting time, and in her mind's eye Wayu saw the seeds begin to unfurl, the young green shoots of corn rising upward to the sun. She knew that the corn would again grow tall and glisten in the morning light, and before long there would be new seed—all part of the annual cycle.

Layered terraces formed the eastern wall of the citadel. They were made of finely hewn blocks of stone, with no mortar. Each granite block fit perfectly with the next, in accordance with Incan custom. Some terraces would be planted with corn, others with quinoa, still others with potatoes—all sacred crops given to Wayu's people by Wiraccocha.

A stone canal captured the free-flowing spring that cascaded down the terraced hillside. The river was 2,000 feet below the citadel, but the sacred spring that flowed endlessly near the Sun Temple brought the gift of water, of life, from the river far below. A small waterfall trickled into the block-lined basin. Warmed by the sun, blessed by the water, Wayu knelt before the waterfall, connecting her heart with the heart of the flowing water, then slowly filled the finely etched jar she carried. She knew the water was a gift from the Cosmic Mother, the *pachamama*.

Carefully balancing the jar, Wayu turned to face the guardian mountain, her beloved Putucusi. Already the morning light filled Putucusi's aura with vivid colors. Closing her eyes, she experienced again the light of the beloved guardian, seeing the same myriad colors within herself. Opening her eyes, Wayu slowly inhaled then exhaled, sending the brilliant light from her heart outward to the *pachamama* and to Putucusi.

Each child of light in the Incan tradition had a guardian mountain, their personal *apu* or mountain spirit. Wayu had known from the time she had first arrived at the residence of the *mamacona* (Machu Picchu) that Putucusi was her *apu*. Rising majestically and lush green from the jungle below, and permeating the surrounding area with its vital energy, Putucusi appeared to touch the clouds that floated above the high citadel. It was effortless for Wayu to dissolve into the heart of Putucusi, to hear from deep within her *apu* the mountain's special teachings. Even at a young age Wayu had been able to listen intently to messages from the Cosmic Mother.

The sacred citadel Machu Picchu was a special school and residence for the most sacred Virgins of the Sun, the *mamacona,* who were in training to serve the *pachamama*. Machu Picchu was the most elite of the *mamacona* schools, but it was far more than that. These young priestesses were the last of an ancient lineage that stretched from the beginning of time. They were the keepers of the old ways, the sacred seed itself.

The training of the *mamacona* was exact and thorough. Like all the young priestesses, Wayu was being trained in the proper use of the receptive vehicles, the inner senses that lead to the development of intuition, deeper knowing, and the sacred arts. A fine weaver, she was now learning the sacred symbols that were incorporated into the weavings. She already knew the prayers for the preparation of ritual foods—corn cakes and *cholla*, the ceremonial drink made of fermented corn. She had also mastered the sacred number systems and could read the sky maps that traced the dances of sacred animals and gods through the night sky. In addition, the most select among the *mamacona*, including Wayu, were trained in the art of speaking without words, the art of listening intently to the Cosmic Mother.

Although it would be many years before she would walk in the steps of the Old One, the one who traveled to the stars and knew the silent language of the gods, young Wayu showed great promise.

Wayu glanced up to the sun gate, the notch in the mountain where the trail down to the valley began. It was the point from which the great mountain peaks surrounding the citadel fanned out in a circle. Father Sun now distanced the sun gate, and Wayu had to hurry to reach her lessons in time.

Even the youngest among the priestesses knew the ancient stories. And the most revered story of all was that of the descent of Wiraccocha, the creator god. It was said that in the beginning, long before the time of the illuminated ones of Wayu's lineage, Wiraccocha first created a dark world. To populate this new world he then created a race of giants, directing them to live in peace and serve him. But they did not obey, so he turned them into stone and sent a great flood called the *uru pachacuti* to transform their world.

Wiraccocha populated the world again, this time creating lamps to give the people light. This creation occurred at the most sacred place in the Incan world, Lake Titicaca. There, Wiraccocha commanded the sun, the moon, and the stars to rise out of the lake and up into the heavens to light the way for the new people. Then, Wiraccocha sent a being created in his likeness as a messenger, and when this being came into the world he brought a sack full of gifts for the people. This new Wiraccocha had great powers: this being was able to transform the shape of the land and give life to all people and to all animals.

The "messenger" Wiraccocha went to the place known as Tiahuanaco, the sacred place of the beginning near the shores of Lake Titicaca. There he created a design in stone of all the people he planned to call forth and nourish in a new world of light. Next, he traveled the mountain paths of the high plateau and called to the new people to emerge from their *paqarinas*, their places of sacred origin, and populate the new world. At the sound of his voice, the gateways opened and the people came forth—some from sacred doorways, some from lakes, others from caves, springs, and trees. To each group he gave a costume, a language, seeds, and sacred songs. Further, he gave all the new people the names of the trees, flowers, and fruits—telling which were for eating and which were for healing.

Wiraccocha admonished the new people to be good, loving, and not to harm others. He then taught them to cultivate the earth, terrace the land, irrigate, and plant the sacred crops of corn, potatoes, and coca. And he gave them sacred arts such as weaving and pottery. Before he left this world, Wiraccocha gave the people of Ollantaytambo, who lived high in the sacred valley, his staff, which was engraved with all his knowledge. Because of this great gift, the town flourished. It was in Ollantaytambo that the first Inca, Manco Capac (the illuminated one) emerged.

When Manco Capac was born, Wiraccocha's staff turned to gold, and the first Incas—four brothers and four sisters—followed the sacred Vilcanota River from Lake Titicaca and emerged from the house of dawn near Ollantaytambo. At the moment of their emergence, they were engendered by a special golden ray of the great sun, illuminating them and causing them to be called "children of the sun."

It had been several years since Wayu and the other *mamacona* had made a pilgrimage over the long, high trail and through the sacred valley to the place of the Pacaritanpu (the place of emergence). It was an arduous journey through the high mountain trails that flanked the breathtaking river. Along the way they had rested in the many sacred sites scattered through the valley. For Wayu, the most spectacular part of the pilgrimage had been seeing the image of Wiraccocha that the ancestors had carved into the sacred mountain near Ollantaytambo. Witnessing his great head of stone awaken in a flood of light, she had experienced how the god-man watched over his people. She and the other *mamacona* had seen the first light of the solstice sun illuminate Wiraccocha's crown chakra and had received his special blessing as the great god-man had awakened. At that moment she had felt deep within herself a stirring she never forgot.

Wayu and the others had journeyed to the very origin place of their people, the house of dawn, the great hidden pyramid from which the first Inca emerged. She had touched the light fields of the *paqarinas* from which her ancestors, the royal Inca, had emerged. Wayu understood the power of her lineage, which came directly from Wiraccocha. Through her veins ran the blood of the great ruling Inca, from Manco Capac to Huayna Capac Inca. She knew that nothing was more powerful than royal blood, the vital heritage of direct descent. Her people were especially chosen by Wiraccocha to carry the seeds of light. They were created to walk in two worlds: the world of form and the world of light. The codes of awakening were held deep within the seeds, and her people's purpose was to travel the pathways of the great initiations (given to the people long ago by Wiraccocha) in order to access those codes. She understood that the solstice dawns and the sacred festivals had engendering powers.

With each dawn light, Wayu felt this ancient legacy awaken clarity within her. She was both an individual carrier of light and also a child of light within a larger collective.

Although few but the *mamacona* knew and practiced the old ways with full potency and awareness, ancient ceremonies of Wiraccocha were still practiced by the people. One of the most important ceremonies of the year, the Activation of the Seed, was close at hand. This ceremony was held when the star cluster called the Pleiades, or the Granary, illuminated the sacred calendar stone at the upper temple plaza and blessed the seeds. It was the greatest of the annual blessings of the sacred seeds, the children of light.

In Wayu's culture, the Pleiades was considered the cosmic star mother who gave to her children the codes of light. She was to them the great Granary, the place in the celestial world where the seeds of light had come from. Wayu had always known where to find the Pleiades in the sky, even feeling the star cluster's presence under a cloudy night sky and throughout the day. So profound was her connection with the Granary that it seemed at times as though its rhythm interlocked with her breath. Each *mamacona* had a special relationship with a celestial deity, and the Granary, the mother seed from which the seeds of light arose, was Wayu's star *apu*. Someday she knew it would show her the way of the stars and the many manifestations of light throughout the universe.

After returning with water, Wayu sat in a circle with the other young priestesses of her age group—six young girls of the royal lineage on the verge of womanhood whose receptive capacities had qualified them for early training. Together their bright tunics formed the colors of the rainbow. They were preparing for the Initiation of the Condor, Wayna Picchu. Wayna Picchu, the great mountain shaped like a condor that looked back at Machu Picchu, embodied the force of feminine energy (in contrast to Machu Picchu's masculine energy). The condor itself was very special to Wayu's people—a symbol of the superior world of divine energies flowing throughout the universe.

Wayu had learned the pathways of all three types of energy in the world—the way of the serpent, the puma, and the condor. She also knew the two perceptions, each a separate reality with its own portals and rules. She had learned that the ordinary world of linear time, was perceived and entered through the five senses. By contrast, the nonordinary world of sacred time, called *yoge*, was perceived and entered through the inner senses. To walk in balance was to hold all aspects of both worlds in the light of the creator.

It was natural and effortless for Wayu to shift into sacred time. She needed to do little more than visualize her beloved Putucusi. She had learned from an early age to listen to the voice of spirit, which manifested in many forms: the rustling of the wind, signs around the sun, the sacred condor's flight, cloud animals, and light within sacred mist.

She was being taught to always pay attention and always control the internal chatter of the mind, an essential element of the training of the *mamacona*. Those who lived within the ordinary world, could let the mind wander aimlessly, wasting the precious gifts of Wiraccocha. But the *mamacona* had to focus attention in order to adhere to the ways of Wiraccocha's lineage—the children of light.

Wayu was being taught to always pay attention to the pull of the inner senses, the doorways to the *yoge*, the nonordinary world. When living in sacred time, she perceived her world from the eyes within and heard the language of silent knowledge. She learned that in moments of heightened awareness she could smell power and even taste the nectars of divine presence.

Wayu realized that messages from her internal senses were unfailingly accurate since they came from the source of truth itself, while messages from her external senses carried only relative truth. Moreover, the world of ordinary reality was like a small box, with external senses forming the boundaries. All perception in this reality was limited by the boundaries the senses placed upon this box.

In addition, the ordinary world was made even smaller by the smells and colors of the emotional fields of the perceiver. She had seen, for example, how smells and colors of fear clouded peoples' perceptual fields and shrank the boundaries of the box, while colors and smells of love expanded boundaries, increasing clarity. Wayu and the other *mamacona* knew the doorways through the box of perception because they lived beyond such limitations. They walked the pathways of the terraced citadel in sacred time, ever alert to the voice of spirit.

By now, the circle of the young priestesses had gathered near the temple of the great priestess, the Old One. Although they were laughing and talking among themselves, there was apprehension in the air. This would be the first of the great initiations of the blood of the Cosmic Mother, one of the most important initiations for entry into womanhood.

Soon the Lightgivers, the teachers charged with preparing the young *mamacona* for initiation, appeared with ceremonial bundles. The Lightgivers had cared for and educated their young companions since the girls were infants. For many of the girls, the coming initiation would change their relationship with the larger community. They knew that the gateways to their individual talents would soon open, allowing them to cultivate those talents in the service of Wiraccocha.

As the time for the ceremony approached, the laughter ceased and the *mamacona* turned their attention inward. Then each received her ceremonial bundle, the gift of the *pachamama*—a conglomerate of sticks, mud, and stones. Wayu reached beneath her tunic for the fine tapestry she had woven for her bundle, a long blue and purple cord that contained a row of interwoven symbols denoting the codes she had learned and the pathways of the *yoge* she had traveled. Her tapestry also contained the symbols for her special *apu*, Putucusi, and her guiding star, the Granary. Next, her Lightgiver instructed the *mamacona* on how to wrap the bundle. She was to pause at each turn and raise her head in prayer to the old condor, Wayna

Picchu. As she ritually wrapped the bundle, her heart became one with the Cosmic Mother, with all of creation, and she opened to the higher light fields of Wiraccocha's love, praying with increasing strength:

> *Beloved Father fill me with your love that I might serve you,*
> *That I might serve the beloved Mother,*
> *That I might be a true vehicle of your love.*

Soon all the *mamacona* were deep in trance, sharing one heart and preparing their sacred bundles for the great ceremony of union. Above them, the mists that rose beyond the summit of Wayna Picchu circled in the morning breezes, becoming gradually more luminous, as if resonating with the prayers.

"When you are finished with your bundles," Wayu's Lightgiver told the girls, "go to the bathing place. There, near the sacred river, carefully bathe yourselves in the warm, healing waters. Prepare yourselves. Then put on your white *yoge* tunics and return to the place of the condor. This is a very special day for all of you. When you are ready, you will receive a blessing by the *pampa mesayog* [an expert healer who works with Earth energies] and his young shaman helper."

Wayu visibly brightened. The great shaman's helper was Cusi, her cousin and her soul's most beloved friend. He was the apprentice to the *pampa mesayog*, the old master who had full knowledge of *pachamama*'s energies and had dedicated himself to the service of the Cosmic Mother and the old ways in this most sacred of citadels. Rarely had the young priestesses received the blessing of the *pampa mesayog*. This occasion was special, for tonight they would enter the cave below Wayna Picchu and offer themselves at the great Temple of the Moon. The preparations had to be perfect; for three days they had fasted, taking only water, and now they were to cleanse themselves and be blessed.

Wayu's Lightgiver caught her eye as the other girls departed. Wayu enfolded herself in her Lightgiver's arms, dissolving the boundaries between them and reentering the dream she had experienced earlier. Again they were at the sacred river near the edge of the jungle, where tall trees formed a canopy high above the rushing torrent, and sunlight filtered prism-like to the water's surface. Her Lightgiver reached deep into the water for the golden light that danced in the recesses, and from the currents of the Vilcanota, the river of the fields of light, she pulled forth flowing rays, showering Wayu in the mystery of spiraling golden light. The light penetrated Wayu's inner senses, purifying her energy body, clearing blockages, and with laser precision, opening new light channels, until her light body shone with the clear radiance of a star in the night sky.

Then Wayu's Lightgiver said, "Do you understand, my beloved Wayu? Your time has come." Wayu nodded, realizing that the dream had signaled the opening of the gateways.

Later, as she hurried down the trail to meet the others, Wayu paused at the sacred river, the place of her dream, and offered prayers of gratitude to the flowing water. There, suddenly, above the canopy in the clear blue sky, she saw the faint form of a condor effortlessly rise and fall on the thermals high above. She knew this would be a day filled with blessings.

Old and bent with his many years, his long white hair pulled back and knotted, the *pampa mesayog* stood before the girls. He could see the pathways of light that made up their luminous bodies, their personal energy fields. He could remove any source of disease before it manifested into form and correct imbalances in a body's current. By the force of his pure intent alone, he was able to irradiate light pathways and remove ancient sources of disharmony and karmic bondage that limited human development.

Like his cousin Wayu, Cusi had come to the high citadel as a small child. Like Wayu he was dark and slight, but he lacked her willowy, ethereal manner. Strong and wiry, at an early age his precociousness had marked him as a candidate for the path of a *pag'o* (shaman). By now he had learned to see with the eyes of the master *mesayog*. Together they traveled the luminous filaments of light in the service of the Cosmic Mother.

It was now Wayu's turn to stand before the *pampa mesayog*. She watched intently as he scanned her energy body. He gestured softly, and she laid down on the flat altar stone. Beside her, Cusi smiled, sending his heart's emanation directly to hers, connecting their luminous filaments until they together became one great channel of light. Smoke rose from the incense burner, mingling with the aromas of the lavender and rosemary oil that the shaman had put on his hands. Again and again, the *pampa mesayog* raised his large black condor feather, cleaning the sacred pathways. Then he gently anointed Wayu's third eye.

Slipping between worlds, Cusi became aware of Wayu's swirling light filaments. Strong, highly refined networks of golden light swirled through her chakras, connecting her with the higher worlds. At this point, the shaman's condor feather pointed to a pathway deep within Wayu's womb, where there was a fibrous knot. Cusi sharpened his focus and perceived the fear that had seized Wayu so long ago. Cusi saw the fear of the child not yet past six blessings of the seed who had been taken from her familiar home and brought to the high citadel. The *pampa mesayog* caught Cusi's eye. Cusi knew what stones the master needed to remove the knot and watched as the *pampa mesayog* worked to dissolve the fear. Finally, the last residue of fear was gone, and Wayu's energy body was unblemished and strong.

Well before Father Sun completed his sky passage, the young *mamacona* and their Lightgivers began the journey down the long but familiar path to the Temple of the Moon in the jungle below. Signs of spring were everywhere; new, tender shoots were beginning to open and delicate leaves were starting to unfurl. The girls knew that each step they took mirrored the passage every *mamacona* before them had made. As Wayu walked, she allowed each breath and footstep to open her heart and soul more fully. She focused on the dream and the signs she had been given this day. When Putacusi's image came into her mind's eye, she slowly sent a line of energy from her womb to her beloved *apu*, connecting her light filaments with the light within the powerful guardian and listening to the mountain's message:

> *Little sister, I shall be with you.*
> *Listen deeply, little sister.*
> *Listen with one heart.*
> *The path will be clear, and the doorways will be open.*

Focusing even more intently, Wayu made her heart one with the others, with the Lightgivers, with all the forms of nature surrounding her. In this state of deep connection with the Cosmic Mother, Wayu approached the portal of the Temple of the Moon. Father Sun's last fiery rays danced upon the horizon. Bending their heads one by one, the young *mamacona*, alert and reverent, entered the dark womb-like space. When her eyes adjusted, Wayu saw before her the silhouette of the Old One.

There in the embrace of Wayna Picchu and under the mask of night, many powerful rituals were performed. Wayu, whose sacred name meant "love song," was charged by pure divinity with such force that each cell within her being became a radiant light-filled crystal. In her physical form, she experienced the full union of the *pachamama* and the *pachamag* (a name for the energy of the Cosmic Father). This lovemaking was so blissful that the stars danced and the sacred mountains wept. And before the first light crossed the sun gate, Wayu had journeyed with the Old One to the faraway filaments of celestial light, through the great gateway, to the very heart of the Milky Way (Mayu). What they learned there could not yet be told, since those teachings were for a later time, for a future incarnation of the light.

The girl Wayu, who had walked down the path to enter the Temple of the Moon at sunset, and the woman Wayu, who in the first light of day walked back to her people at the citadel, were not the same. All who saw her knew that her time had come. She would someday be the Old One's successor, a great *kuraq* (visionary). Because there was still much for Wayu to learn, following the ceremony Wayu and her Lightgiver moved their belongings to the Old One's secluded residence. Wayu's days were now filled with lessons about specific traditions that required heightened and steady focus. The days were long, but a new vitality filled her body. Her nights were now spent in the dream pathways of the night sky—in the Old One's embrace. At first Wayu missed the camaraderie she had shared with the other young girls, but from the time of her childhood she had always known her path was a different one and that she belonged to Wiraccocha, not to a life of family.

Shortly after Wayu's initiation, Cusi was sent by the *pampa mesayog* to begin apprenticeships with other powerful *mesayogs* in the valley and beyond. Wayu missed Cusi and longed for his return. Since childhood they had played together in their special cave on the path to the sun gate, where the sharing of visions and dreams had forged a deep soul connection between them. While Wayu waited in eagerness for Cusi's return and wondered what he was learning in the world far below, she understood that only distance separated them. She knew that when Cusi came back they would again share their visions and their dreams. She did not realize that it would be years before she saw Cusi again.

One moon had nearly passed since Wayu's initiation. Preparations were now underway throughout the citadel for the great Festival of the Activation of the Seed, one of only a few occasions where outsiders were welcomed to the sacred ceremonies at the home of the *mamacona*. For this annual festival, people from throughout the sacred valley below carried their seeds many arduous miles to the high citadel to receive a special blessing. And for this fortuitous day the great Inca ruler himself sent his special emissary, the high priest from the royal city of Cuzco, to attend the ceremonies in the sacred home of the *mamacona*.

At the time of the activation, the light from the Granary (the Pleiadean star cluster) reappeared prior to sunrise and shone upon the people, marking the special stone near the *intihuatana* (a large calendric stone that used shadows cast by the sun), in the great ceremonial plaza. At the same moment, the light of the Pleiades flooded the windows of the Sun Temple near the waterfall. The sunrise at this special time also had profound power, making foretelling possible. It was well known that at the very moment when the Granary reappeared before sunrise and sent its blessings for the year to the sacred seed, something auspicious occurred. This was the time each year when Wiraccocha himself spoke to the Old One and showed her the path of the future.

The eighth Inca ruler was historically known to be prophetic. He had foreseen the decline of the Inca empire but had tried to keep the prophecy hidden. Now, the current Inca ruler and his advisors in the priesthood were again obsessed with the prophecies—and for good reason. Wayu and the other *mamacona* knew of the mysterious, dreadful prophecies foretelling that they and the long line of Inca, the blood of the children of light that came from the very beginning of time itself, were endangered. Although it appeared as though their entire lineage was now near its end, Wayu and the Old One knew that things were not as they appeared.

It was with a great burden that the high priest of the royal Inca court himself journeyed from Cuzco to the high citadel of the *mamacona*. His small escort party was drawn from the finest of the royal army, all loyal warriors. As they made their way down from the sun gate, Wayu and the other *mamacona* saw the fear they carried within them and that even the high priest of the Inca himself was trapped within the box of limited perception.

That night around the fire Wayu listened as the high priest spoke in hushed tones to the Old One.

"The signs," he said, "were everywhere. We have seen comets in the heavens. Just last week earthquakes shook the central plaza of the great royal residence. Even now the moon is circled with rings of fire."

Wayu pulled her blanket more tightly around her small frame and listened intently.

"I have heard reports of landings of strange bearded white foreigners in floating cities at the ocean's edge," the priest said. "The story foretold in the night sky so long ago, can no longer be denied."

The peasantry was on the verge of panic, and there was great tension among the royal court. The great Incan empire seemed on the verge of collapse. Only a powerful sign from Wiraccocha would bring calm. The priest leaned closer to the Old One, and Wayu could barely hear his hushed voice:

"When the Granary appears and Wiraccocha speaks to you," he whispered, "the report must be positive. The royal Inca desperately need your cooperation. I will do anything you request," the priest pleaded.

Wayu saw the Old One's face harden, her body become rigid. Although Wayu understood little about the world or the political concerns of the royal Inca court, she knew that the Old One would only speak the truth. In these short weeks with the Old One, her understanding had grown enormously. She now comprehended many of the old teachings. She had journeyed far beyond the constraints of linear time, truly stepping outside of it. She knew that she was nothing but energy and that energy could neither be created nor destroyed. She understood that she was for all time one with the light of the creator. As a child of light she was Wiraccocha's reflection here in physical form. She and the Old One were servants of the light here in this time and space.

The day came for the Festival of the Activation of the Seed. This was the time when the light of the Granary shone brightly upon the seeds below. The high priest of the royal court and his entourage appeared dressed in their finest garments, interwoven with gold and silver threads and accentuated with jewelry of precious stones. Their large dangling golden earrings, the mark of the Inca royalty, glittered in the predawn light.

The high priest held the red-tasseled fringe of the ruling Inca. Dressed in their simple *yoge* tunics, Wayu and the Old One, along with the others, watched the early morning sky just before sunrise as the Granary reappeared, bringing its blessing to the people.

Wayu saw with the eyes of the Old One and heard within herself the voice of Wiraccocha. She knew the seed would now be scattered by the winds of change. This would be a time of much disruption, a time for moving inward. Hidden deep within the earth, the seed would lie dormant through a dark, cold night, until it was awakened by a new sun. Then the gateways would again open, and the children of light would return.

Years passed, and occasional visitors to the high citadel brought disturbing news of the outer world—tales of war and devastation at the borders of the empire. One day Wayu saw a tall, thin young man walking with great confidence down the path from the sun gate, and her heart leaped as she recognized Cusi. As she watched him come closer to the village and noticed how handsome he had become, she felt a new longing deep within her womb, a strange physical sensation that left her feeling uneasy and confused.

Cusi was welcomed back into the community by the Old One and by a proud *pampa mesayog*. He and Wayu greeted each other shyly, both surprised by the powerful physical attraction they felt and uncertain of how to relate to each other now that they were adults. For a few weeks they saw little of each other since Cusi spent his days with the *pampa mesayog*, far from the women's temple. Some nights Wayu and the Old One joined the men around a fire at the *intihuatana,* where a reserved and seemingly self-contained Cusi gave detailed reports of the increasing collapse of the outer world.

Wayu seldom left the women's temple or the residence of the Old One. She was troubled by the emotions Cusi had triggered in her. Nothing had prepared her for these feelings, not even the secrets of the old ways that the Old One had taught her or their nighttime journeys into the center of light itself. When she did join in the gatherings, she watched Cusi from a distance, turning quickly away when he caught her eye. On occasions when he attempted to seek her out, she fled, unable to face him in such inner turmoil.

Although the Old One immediately understood the cause of Wayu's discomfort and Cusi's reserve, she waited until Wayu grew increasingly restless. A few weeks after Cusi's homecoming, when Wayu returned from dinner at the women's temple, the Old One, the *pampa mesayog,* and Cusi sat waiting for her around the fire. Then the old masters talked candidly to Wayu and Cusi.

"Your yearnings for physical union are understandable," the *mesayog* coached. "You are free to choose your future. However, because you are both of royal lineage and because of your vows of celibacy, the situation between you has to be resolved soon.

"There are many ways to explore the path of *yanantin* [the harmonic relationship of opposites], aside from the mere physical union of man and woman," the priest continued. "Each initiate needs to master both their male and female energies as an essential part of their training. You are free to leave your training and vows of celibacy, but if you stay at the citadel, your next level of training will involve the dynamic blending of male and female energy—on a higher level and for the good of the community as a whole."

The mesayog handed Wayu and Cusi a bag containing provisions. "Go to the cave of *pachamama* and do not to return until you have reached a decision."

Somewhat startled by the abrupt and unexpected command of the *pampa mesayog,* Wayu and Cusi set out on the moonlit path to the cave of the Cosmic Mother. On the way, Wayu glanced toward her beloved *apu,* Putucusi, which was crowned with moonlight. She released the heavy, confused energy she felt and opened pathways within her to the *yoge.* Immediately she realized the absurdity of their situation and began to laugh. Cusi soon joined in, and the tension between them dissipated. Soon they chatted like the good friends they were. They both knew that they were not interested in abandoning training and would, instead, learn to work with the new energies emerging in them. They spent a joyful night in the cave sharing experiences and what they had learned during the last three years.

In time, Wayu found new ways to integrate duality. As her inner male energies developed, she became more expressive and decisive. When she felt confusion or negative emotions, she challenged her inner turmoil until she attained clarity. Gradually, her inner polarities were brought into harmony. Like the great androgynous Wiraccocha, Wayu learned that true leadership requires the harmonious interaction of both male and female energies. And Cusi, absorbed in the heart of the *pachamama*, found his own path to the sacred.

Years passed, then decades. Wayu became old, each year taking on more of the Old One's duties. As the Old One left this world, Wayu embraced her frail body. She had taught Wayu everything; they had become as one being. When the last glimmer of luminosity left the Old One, Wayu traveled with her through the familiar portals one last time. Wayu watched while the Old One became pure radiance merging with the light between the stars.

After the Old One returned to the stars Wayu took her place, preserving the traditional sacred ways. Although there were many changes in the exterior world, the high citadel remained untouched and increasingly isolated. Emissaries of the royal Inca no longer journeyed the pathways above the sacred river, the farmers from the valley no longer brought their seeds for annual blessings, and precocious young girls were no longer sent to the high citadel to become *mamacona*.

Eventually, it was as if the outer world ceased to exist. Those at the citadel planted corn and potatoes, offered prayers, and felt the blessings of Great Sun as they had always done. Wayu, Cusi, and the *mamacona* grew old together in the service of the *pachamama*.

Wayu knew that someday there would be a future incarnation of the light, that the sixth sun would awaken the light codes hidden deep within the human form. To prepare for such a time, Wayu and Cusi watched the night sky, tracked the shadows that fell on the *intihuatana*, listened to the rhythm of the Granary as it rose and set above the citadel, and made their calculations accordingly.

As the chaos of the physical world continued to encroach on the realm of the sacred, Wayu and Cusi realized that the *huacas*, the holy places that held the ancient gateways, were now in danger. These holy places had to be protected since, at a future time, the secrets they held would again be revealed. Someday the children of light would again learn to dance in wholeness and evoke the higher order. Solemnly and dutifully, Wayu and Cusi determined that the doorways to the energy fields had to be sealed and hidden. In communion with the *apus*, Wayu traveled the pathways of light, making sure that sacred guardians were aligned, the holy places sealed, and the codes to the ancient glyphs hidden. She knew that the old knowledge would be preserved, for now only those who had the key could access the gateways.

Before Wayu passed from this world, she carefully sealed the entrances to the sacred citadel. Machu Picchu would remain hidden for hundreds of years. Its energy fields and spiritual forces would await the return of the children of light, who would again mirror the divine and walk in perfect balance, in perfect *ayni*. Wayu had seen long ago that the next incarnation of light would be the true *chakarunas,* the bridge people, the new luminous ones who would bring the full potential of divine light to all humanity.

In 1911, explorer Hiram Bingham discovered what he called the "Lost City of the Inca," Machu Picchu. A new road had recently been built along the Urubamba River (the Vilcanota) near Ollantaytambo. After natives had told him about a ruin high in the mountains, he and his guides scaled a 2,000-foot slope and found the path to the ruins, which had been concealed beneath mountain vegetation for hundreds of years. The high citadel, which was the spectacular sanctuary of the Inca world, had never been found by the Span-ish conquistadors and was still intact, including the intihuatana.[1] *Many years later it was opened to the public.*

It was verified that the enchanting and extraordinarily beautiful ancient site had once been an important ceremonial center and the home of the mamacona, *the Virgins of the Sun. Researchers found skeletons (primarily of women) entombed at the site. The skeleton of an old woman was found in a tomb near a building believed to be the residence of the high priestess.*

2

SEEDINGS
OF DIVINE
CONSCIOUSNESS

THE WORLD OF THE MAMACONA WAS IMMERSED IN MYTH and thus animated in a way long lost to contemporary consciousness. They lived within a complex, multilevel cosmology in which everything was alive and a source of information. The *mamacona* lived according to the ancient knowledge that everything in the world was conscious, a belief they expressed in every thought and action. They lived beyond what has become known as the veil of separation, modern humanity's illusion that the mundane physical world is the only reality.

The *mamacona's* creation myths and legends stretched back to the beginnings of time—revealing, from one generation to the next, direct interaction between men and deities. To the *mamacona* Wiraccocha was still an active, engendering force. Thus their legends were not merely stories but vivid evidence of the light of divinity making itself known through form. As children of the light, they understood that they were part of divine expression, the sacred seed engendered by the creator.

Wiraccocha's Legacy—Children of Light
The *mamacona* also understood how tremendously important it was that their people were god-seeds. They knew that the seeds of the divine had

been planted deep within the hearts of the children of light and that their people were the last of a seeded race. In Wayu's time, although many traditions had been lost, the potency of the lineage remained. When at each sunrise the Old One called forth the name of Wiraccocha, she invoked within herself the codes of light that connected the higher world with the world of form. She evoked the living blueprint of light itself, the source of the divine consciousness that was hidden in human form.

According to Andean mythology, the creator god Wiraccocha had come in human form from the higher worlds. Although each regional tradition has its own version of the creation story, all are remarkably similar. It is said that long ago when the world was without light, Wiraccocha came to a place above the dark waters of Lake Titicaca. There, high in the Andes near the Peruvian-Bolivian border, this god-man called forth the sun, moon, and stars and placed them above Lake Titicaca. He then created the tribes of the Andes, each with its own place of emergence, language, and customs. Every tribe was given a holy statute that held divine power and could evoke the seed of the lineage that directly connected the divine and the human. In Quechua, the language spoken by the Inca and still in use in the high Andes, this statute was called a *waka*.

Wiraccocha then spoke gently to his people, the seeds, telling them to do good, to be loving and charitable to all, and to bring no injury to another. He then taught them how to live harmoniously and to bring forth prosperity, showing them how to terrace, engineer systems of irrigation, and grow sacred crops.

The myths, as told by Incan record keepers (the *quipucamayocs*), relate that in about 200 B.C., light entered the world in the form of the god-man Wiraccocha. The civilization known as Tiahuanaco that developed in the high Andes reached its zenith as a sacred center about A.D. 600. Historical records show evidence of a sudden catalyst of enormous power affecting Andean life in about 200 B.C., resulting in a rapid development of "vertical archipelagoes" and a complex agricultural order which unified the people of the high-altitude valleys and mountains into a single, interdependent, prosperous community.[1]

Today not much is known about this great culture because there is no written record. Only ruins remain, which were repeatedly pillaged by early treasure seekers long before the arrival of archaeologists. However, based upon the remnants of artwork and materials recovered from burial sites, archaeologists believe that this civilization extended from the Peruvian coast to the Bolivian highlands, had a highly evolved religious base, and was peaceful, apparently expanding its base through the sharing of knowledge. It is believed that many of the Incan customs and myths were derived from the "golden age" of Tiahuanaco.

Located about 12 miles from Lake Titicaca, just over the Peruvian border in Bolivia, are the ruins of perhaps the most spectacular archaeological monument in all of South America. This structure, which is believed to have been built by the Tiahuanaco, is known as the Gateway to the Sun. It is a large gateway above which is carved the image of the androgynous god-man Wiraccocha. Solar rays emanate from his head and golden tears of light appear to fall from his eyes.

In Wayu's time, long after Wiraccocha had left this world, his ways were still held sacred by those who worked the earth and by the priestesses dedicated to maintaining tradition. Each year the faithful gathered for the Festival of the Return of the Pleiades. On the dawn of each solstice and each equinox, they came to receive the special blessing of the Father Sun.

Each year on December 22, their summer solstice, the Inca also celebrated an important festival dedicated to the young men who had reached manhood, the Festival of Capac Rayni, or the Festival of the Kings. On this day, young men were formally accepted into the community, and, as was the royal Inca custom, their ears were pierced with large gold earrings. The Capac Rayni was a time to bless and give thanks for the crops that provided daily nourishment, as well as for the seeds of the royal lineage, the divine god-seeds. The festival was an expression of the Incan multilevel cosmology. For as the ceremony was conducted in Cuzco, further up the sacred valley near the town of Ollantaytambo, the morning solstice sun lit the top of the head, the crown chakra, of the massive form of Wiraccocha carved into the mountain—symbolically awakening divine consciousness. Shortly thereafter, the light lit up the granary, the part of the temple which held the seeds reserved for planting.

The Inca conducted most of their rituals at dawn because they believed that the first light was the most potent, bringing with it a great blessing and knowledge from divine sources. Their rituals had a dual purpose: to enhance the spiritual well-being of the people and strengthen seeds, grains, and flocks.[2]

The equinoxes, solstices, and the return of the Pleiades were observed and celebrated with absolute precision by the Inca and other indigenous peoples around the world. They built massive and complex calendars which recorded the exact progression of the sun and accurately marked the precise moment of the spring and winter solstices. The date of the return of the Pleiades, the solstices, the equinoxes, as well as other holy days, were critically important and spiritually significant to indigenous peoples who believed that at or before dawn on these holy days a special blessing was available. Although many contemporary researchers of Andean culture believe these dates were important because they indicated when the people should plant their crops, it is also known that these dates had a greater spiritual significance.

The importance of light as a spiritual force is emphasized in the Inca creation story, wherein Wiraccocha gives his second creation the added advantage of light. He directed the sun, stars, and moon to come forth from Lake Titicaca and placed them in the sky so they might give light to his children. This light was not ordinary light but the light of divine consciousness that manifested in form. For the Inca, physical light had engendering qualities, awakening the light codes buried in the human form. The Incan creation story underscores the notion of divine engendering by light, by relating that when the children of the sun emerged from the sacred doorways between the worlds and stepped into dawn on the solstice morning, they were showered with fertile, golden light.[3] Only then did they become the Inca, which means "illuminated ones."

Role of the Pleiadian Star Cluster

The Pleiadian star cluster played a key role in Incan and Mayan mythology.[4] An intriguing fact about this star cluster has to do with Mayan knowledge about the number of stars in the cluster. The Pleiades, also called the Seven Sisters, was supposedly so named because only seven of its stars are visible to the naked eye, although it actually contains some four hundred stars. Interestingly, among the Maya, one of the names for the Pleiades was "the four hundred boys."[5] Since most of these stars cannot be seen, it is not known how the Maya could have known the approximate number of stars.

The Pleiades was particularly important to the Inca in determining the seasons. At certain times during the year, specific stars or constellations are not visible from the earth because they appear too close to the sun, but they reappear once they "clear" the sun's brilliance. The date of the reappearance of a star is known as its heliacal rise. On the day of the return of the Pleiades, which was calculated precisely by the Inca, the star cluster was again visible just before sunrise after a period of invisibility. This was the date of the Festival of the Return of the Pleiades, which was an important tool for calendric measurement, used by the Inca to note the exact time of the solstice.[6] In the time of the Inca, the heliacal rise of the Pleiades was always 30 days before the solstice, allowing the Inca to plan for the time of the solstice, which could not be calculated by watching the sun.

So important was the Pleiades to the Incan worldview that the star cluster provided a basis for the Incan calendar. In the ancient city of Cuzco, some forty-two invisible lines known as *seques*, or rays, surrounded the great Temple of the Sun, extending all the way to the horizon. Each *seque* passed through or near a shrine, or small statute, known as a *waka*. According to the creation myth, the *wakas* held the power of the lineage and connected the people directly to their origin, the stars. There were between seven and nine *wakas* per *seque*, for a total of 328. According to Spanish chronicles, each *waka* represented one day of the year.[7] However, there were only 328 *wakas*, not 365. Tom Zuidema and Gary Urton, ethnoastronomers who have studied the Inca, point out that the difference can be accounted for by noting that the Pleiades is invisible in the latitude above Cuzco during the missing 37 days.

The ancient astronomers of Wayu's time called the Pleiades the "great Granary." In Quechua, the Pleiades is referred to as *collca*, which means granary, while the Quechua term used in northern Bolivia for the Pleiades is *coto*, which means a handful of seeds.[8] This is also how the Maya saw the Pleiades.

In veiled language, esoteric teachings tell us that the divine aspect of the human form came from the stars and that the cluster of the Pleiades provided the blueprints for human consciousness. These blueprints may be thought of as actual codes of light that have been implanted within the human form.[9] These light codes can be seen as divine thought forms that provide the catalysts that awaken in mankind the light that brings higher consciousness.

A helpful analogy for this human process is the seed of any common plant. For example, the seed of any flower has within it a hidden code contained in the plant's DNA that becomes activated under certain conditions: time of year, amount of sunlight and moisture. The code causes the seed to sprout, grow, flower, bear fruit, produce seed, and then repeat the same cycle. Similarly, the light codes within the human form may be viewed as spiritual DNA, as the inner forces that trigger the process of enlightenment. The ultimate maturation of the god-seed in each human being is divinity, an example of which is Christ consciousness.

Esoteric texts trace the seed of illumination to the great Granary, the Pleiades. In antiquity, in cultures across the world, the Pleiades was called the "seedbed," the "cradle," and "the throne of the codes." Esotericists such as J. J. Hurtak believe that the divine imprint, the prephysical garment of light that enabled human physical form to hold divine consciousness, is associated with the Pleiades.[10]

The prephysical garment of light is similar to the idea of divine intent. It was through divine intent that divine consciousness could enter the womb of matter, the physical parameters of our reality. This is the reality we perceive with the five senses—one that exists within linear time, is measurable, and energetically very dense. Since matter is not readily penetrated by light, the sacred energy that came from the Pleiades provided the necessary interface for more refined energies in the form of light to be held in the three-dimensional world, the physical plane. Thus it helped to join the refined energies of the light of consciousness with the denser energies of matter.

In the creation stories of people all over the world, there are many references to intervention by divine sources from outside our solar system.[11] In addition to alluding to the Pleiades in such contexts, some esoteric texts also refer to the significance of the constellation Orion. According to Hurtak, Orion provided the pure light bodies upon which the sacred light codes from the Pleiades were programmed. Orion is also said to be the source of all "gnosis"—the spiritual power of the divine force itself.[12]

Human Seeds of Light

According to some esoteric accounts, such as Hurtak's and Sumerian and Babylonian creation myths from which later Hebraic creation myths may have derived, a purpose of the spiritual human, the seed, was to create a new species capable of carrying the light of higher consciousness.[13] This species is known as the Adamic Race, or the Adam Kadmon. Gnostic and other texts emphasize that the Adam Kadmon is a continually evolving species of light made in "the image and similitude" of the Elohim (angels). Hopi and Mayan myths also refer to the concept of a continually evolving creation.[14]

Many of these traditions tell of androgynous god-like beings known in early Hebraic accounts as the Elohim. Within the hierarchy of the spiritual world, the Elohim are considered mighty angels who embody high intelligence and creative powers, and who sit at the right hand of God himself. Some sources say the Elohim are connected with the constellation Orion.[15]

The Sumerian and Babylonian tablets, which stem from one of the oldest civilizations on this planet, describe strangers called "serpents," who were "shining and radiant ones" with large brilliant eyes and luminous faces. It was these beings who allegedly brought to the Sumerian and Babylonian cultures the seeds of civilization.[16]

Later Hebraic texts, said to be written by a scribe named Enoch, describe beings known as the "Shining Ones" who arrived in what is now Lebanon some 10,000 years ago.[17] The writings attributed to Enoch are no longer found in the Old Testament and are considered among the apocrypha, or "hidden" texts, along with the "heretical" Gnostic texts. Accounts of these supernatural beings eventually made their way into Hebrew angel lore, where the beings came to be called the Seraphim, the highest order of angels and "fiery flying serpents of lightening."[18]

It is interesting to note, as pointed out by modern angelologist Malcom Godwin, that the root word *El* (contained in *Elohim*), is an ancient term with common origins in many languages. For example, in Sumerian *El* means "brightness or shining"; in Babylonian *Ellu* means "the shining one"; in English *elf* means "shining being"; and in Anglo-Saxon *aelf* means "radiant being."[19]

The concept of luminous creator beings is also found in the Tibetan *Book of Dzyan*, which describes luminous ones who produced "form from no form," "shone like the sun," and were "blazing divine dragons of serpent wisdom."[20] In addition, as we will see, there are accounts of intervention by luminous god-men who were also called serpents throughout Mesoamerica and Peru.

The Elohim, who at various times have been known as "god-men," "space beings," the "older brothers," and "world teachers," have a long history of intercession with planet Earth. To them, Earth is a sacred garden in which many plantings have been made. They are the grand gardeners responsible for numerous propagations of the seed, and they have made many attempts to upgrade the intelligence and spiritual consciousness of the human form. We may both metaphorically and literally be the seed of the Elohim.

Those of us shaped by the Judeo-Christian worldview have been taught that "man is made into the image and similitude of God."[21] While this is surely true, it is important to remember that the work of creation is not yet complete. The work of the Elohim in seeding the consciousness of the spiritual race of man is an ongoing process.

Careful reading of the above-cited biblical passage actually supports the idea of a continuously evolving consciousness. The word *into* suggests that evolution is ongoing, while the word *similitude* tells us that we were made like the creator (in this context the Elohim), implying that in the physical dimension matter has the ability to hold light. This is a profound realization that means we all have the potential to hold and radiate light.[22]

Lemurian and Atlantean Seedbeds

Myths of many cultures tell of lost ancient civilizations. The legendary civilizations of Lemuria and Atlantis are still part of the human collective memory. Whether the ancient worlds of Lemuria and Atlantis existed apart from myth does not matter, since the idea is now a permanent part of the human experience and has shaped our vision of the present and future.

Esoteric accounts tell us that the first seedings of the Elohim occurred in the ancient worlds of prehistory, some 36,000 years ago or earlier.[23] In these ancient traditions, the world of Lemuria or "Mu" (a large island continent in the Pacific Ocean near South America) was the first world, or Mother world.

According to legend, the Lemurians were luminous beings who had direct contact with higher intelligence. Reputedly, they had collective perception—that is, they had shared thoughts, could perceive as a whole, and were very telepathic. In their time, human consciousness had not yet been fully integrated into dense physical reality, and the Lemurians existed more in the ethereal than in the physical realm. They had not yet left the Garden of Eden.

Peruvian folklore is filled with references to the Lemurians. It is believed that the ruins of Tiahuanaco sit upon the ruins of a far older culture that existed long before the Andes were thrust upward. According to legend, Tiahuanaco, which was once at sea level, represents the remains of the continent of Lemuria—submerged prior to 30,000 B.C. as a result of massive geological catastrophes. The implication is that the Tiahuanaco, from whom the Inca claim to be descended, were a remnant seed of the Lemurians.

Another seeding is said to have occurred in the lost world of Atlantis, the physical remains of which reputedly lie in the Atlantic Ocean. Some accounts place Atlantis in the Bermuda triangle, while others claim Atlantis was in the Mediterranean and suggest the Greek island of Santorini[24] is a vestige of the lost world. The Atlanteans were said to be a highly advanced race with a civilization unlike any the world had previously seen. Many believe that when their homeland was destroyed, the Atlanteans migrated to Egypt, Mesoamerica, India, and Tibet, seeding many new civilizations.

Virtually all the peoples of Mesoamerica have stories about how their earliest ancestors came from a land to the east in boats after a massive flood. Although the theory of a continental split is largely accepted, there is also considerable scientific documentation of major world flooding over 10,000 years ago at the end of the last Ice Age. For example, University of Miami geologist Cesare Emiliani has through extensive core drilling in the Gulf of Mexico indisputably established that the entire Yucatán Peninsula was flooded about 12,000 years ago. Moreover, it has been determined that the Gulf of Mexico rose as much as 130 feet above the present sea level when the last glaciers melted.[25]

Clearly, in ancient times there were numerous catastrophes on earth that would have profoundly affected all human, animal, and plant life. However, it is important to recognize that the flood commonly referred to in origin stories throughout Mesoamerica and Peru may have been a psychological rather than a physical event.[26] From a mythological perspective, a flood may represent a period in which the higher consciousness of a group is submerged in the waves of the unconscious, a period of sudden transformation of a cultural worldview during which ancient knowledge is cast aside for new beliefs, or a time in which evolutionary progress is impeded.[27]

It is indisputable that some physical or psychological event occurred in early human history of which we have only a vague and collective memory. We may never be able to prove what actually occurred since our knowledge of ancient human history has long been submerged beneath the floodwaters of time. And although archaeologists continue to search for Lemuria and Atlantis, it may be futile to debate whether these ancient worlds actually existed, since they are a well-established part of human mythology and serve the important purpose of translating ancient wisdom into modern consciousness.

Seeded Cultures of Mesoamerica and Peru

There is substantial evidence of cultures (known as the Olmec, the Teotihuacán, the Zapotec, the Maya, the Tiahuanaco, and somewhat later the Inca) being seeded simultaneously in Mesoamerica and Peru. Highly evolved spiritually, these cultures were allegedly ruled by priest-kings and god-men to whom they trace their lineage, and all considered themselves children of light.

Although most original manuscripts of ancient cultures found in Mesoamerica were destroyed by zealous Spanish clerics who considered these records pagan aberrations, a few survived this fanaticism.[28] One of the most important, the *Popol Vuh*, is considered to be the Bible of Mayan mythology. Others provide fragmentary information about the early people of Mesoamerica. For example, although perhaps later in time, the *Books of Chilan Balam* discusses the origin of the first inhabitants of the Yucatán, called Chanes or the "People of the Serpent," who allegedly came in boats with their leader Zamma in the year A.D. 219.

Zamma is described as the "Serpent of the East," a god-like man. He was said to be a powerful healer who, like the Christ figure, could cure by laying on of hands and revive the dead.[29] In the myths and stories of the Yucatán region there are many references to the "people of the serpent."[30] The serpents, sometimes called *nagas,* appear to make up an archaic mystery school with leaders considered to be spiritually powerful initiates. Some scholars believe that *nagas* were survivors of Atlantis and may have had extraterrestrial origins.[31] Even today there are groups in Mesoamerica that trace their lineage to the legendary serpents, such as the Tacuate of the state of Oaxaca, who maintain a strong *nagual* tradition.

In this context, it is interesting to examine some of the various esoteric meanings of the word "serpent". The term sometimes refers to the kundalini energy (the yogic life force that lies coiled at the base of the spine until it is aroused and sent to the head to trigger enlightenment) that rises serpentlike up the human chakra system. A chakra, according to Hinduism and Tantric Buddhism, is a focal point where psychic forces and bodily functions merge and interact. There are some 88,000 chakras in the body. Six major ones are located along the spinal column, and a seventh, called the crown chakra, is found at the top of the skull. The lowest of the seven is found at the base of the spine and is associated with the mysteries of divine potency attributed to the force of kundalini. This force is believed to be a cosmic energy that lies latent within every body and can be visualized as a serpent coiled at the base of the spine. Various yogic techniques can raise this energy up the spine, chakra by chakra, to the crown where self-illumination is then said to occur.[32] There is documentation that ancient initiatory rites around the world were intended to enhance this process.[33] Moreover, according to some Sumerian and biblical stories, the word "serpent" is derived from the word *nahash,* which means " he who finds things out, he who can decipher."[34]

As we will see, the indigenous people of Mesoamerica clearly had access to ancient sacred knowledge, although its source is unknown. Figurines and other depictions of the early priest-kings of Mesoamerica found in the La Venta area—an ancient Olmec settlement located near the border of modern Tabasco and Veracruz states—and elsewhere show tall, bearded, long-robed men in headdresses with features that have Semitic, Phoenician, Negroid, or Chinese characteristics.[35] Even Quetzalcoatl— a chief Toltec and Aztec god-man identified with rain, Venus, and the morning star, and represented by a feathered serpent—was sometimes depicted as a tall, bearded being. It is well known that the indigenous people of Mesoamerica, whose ancestors allegedly came to this continent over the Bering Strait, did not have the genetic capacity to grow beards, were not tall, and did not have African, European, or distinctly Oriental features. Although we do not know who these priest-kings or god-men were or where they came from, they apparently introduced the people of Mesoamerica to the great initiations and the path of the great mysteries.

At Monte Albán, a ruined city of the Zapotec near Oaxaca in southern Mexico, there is a collection of very old stelae, figures in various postures engraved on stone slabs. Evidence of the use of the Mayan long count (the system used on stelae to accurately describe a given date) was found on these slabs. This evidence dated the slabs to at least 600 B.C. They also display a sophisticated knowledge of the human chakra system and the use of kundalini. They portray human figures in various states of ecstasy as if dancing between worlds and are likely related to powerful initiation rites.

Early explorations of Mesoamerican cultures have yielded further insights into ancient traditions and their use of sacred knowledge. Augustus Le Plongeon, a Frenchman, was the first European adventurer to gain the trust of the early Maya. Along with his wife Alice he spent some 12 years living among them in the 1870s. During this time the people shared with him secret lore for which the Spanish had burned many of their ancestors at the stake. Le Plongeon learned that the Maya still practiced magic and described shamans who disappeared and reappeared like Carlos Casteneda's don Juan and who made strange objects appear and disappear.[36] Such practices are not unlike those of the *siddhis* or powers of the great yogis of contemporary India. Le Plongeon describes the activities of the Mayan shamans in the following manner:

"Sometimes the place where they were operating would seem to shake as if an earthquake were occurring, or whirl around and around as if being carried away by a tornado. Sometimes they [the shamans] appeared to be bathed in bright and resplendent light, and flames seemed to issue from the walls only to be extinguished by invisible hands in the most profound obscurity where flashes of lightning made the dark appear darker."[37]

Such stories of the miraculous raise serious questions about who these early people were. Although many theories exist that suggest the peoples of Mesoamerica and Peru were descendants of Atlantis or Lemuria, questions about the identity of these early people have never been definitively answered. Yet, despite limited knowledge, there is a sizable amount of information (including the modern dating of the ruins) that lends credence to the idea that Mesoamerican civilizations were remnants of far earlier seedings.

One case in point is evidence suggested by William Niven, a mining engineer who worked for a Mexican corporation and who, between 1910 and 1930, discovered the remains of two separate prehistoric civilizations near Mexico City. Based on the strata these ruins were found in, they are believed to be over 50,000 years old. However, since there was no other evidence of any civilization this old, conventional academians entirely ignored his findings. But believers in the existence of Atlantis became very excited and rapidly popularized his findings to support their theories.

The most dramatic of Niven's discoveries were 2,600 stone tablets with strange paintings or pictographs, found in a hamlet near Mexico City. Based on the strata in which they were found, the tablets were thought to be between 12,000 and 50,000 years old. Some tablets included figures that depicted certain Masonic gestures and symbols that were still practiced by Masons in Niven's time. These figures demonstrated a knowledge of ancient mysteries that remain the basis of the great mystery schools.[38]

Although the origin of early Mesoamerican civilizations remains a mystery, we know that in areas throughout Mesoamerica and Peru, cultures appeared rapidly and almost simultaneously, quickly developing very advanced civilizations. Unlike anything the world had previously seen, these civilizations were both spiritually evolved and materially stable. The people of these civilizations built huge pyramids and massive ceremonial centers and had a highly developed knowledge of mathematics and astronomy. Then, as mysteriously as these apparently unconnected but advanced civilizations had appeared, they disappeared—all about the same time. At Teotihuacán, Palenque, Monte Albán, Tiahuanaco, and throughout Mesoamerica as early as A.D. 650, many of the most extraordinary temples, pyramids, and ceremonial centers were abandoned—destroyed by their builders and in some cases actually buried. According to folklore, the priest kings disappeared one day, making the journey across the great cosmic river and bridge in the Milky Way to the land of the gods.

Other Attempts to Create People of Light

There is evidence that divine seedings were not limited to Peru and Mesoamerica. In Egypt, the Great Pyramid and the Sphinx are thought by some researchers to be far more ancient than 4,000 years old. Irrespective of their ages, it is widely speculated that the early cultures of both Mesoamerica and Egypt were remnants of the civilization of Atlantis. Moreover, more esoteric sources suggest that early priest-kings who ruled these civilizations were divine beings like the mythical Elohim.[39]

Some people believe that another seeding by the Elohim occurred some 6,000 years ago in the Middle East. It is speculated that after years of wandering, these seeded people eventually came to Egypt and became known as the Hebrews.[40] The purpose of this seeding was to again create a people of light who would have a higher capacity to think universally and a physical structure able to perceive higher vibrational frequencies than the mass of humanity.

It is interesting to note that the great Hebrew leader Moses was said to be a high initiate who came from Heliopolis, the city of the sun. The name Moses, or Muse, was a name meaning "sent," and was given to the high initiates. The Greek variation translates as the "son of the sun" which was the appellation given to the Inca.[41] Moses appeared at the end of the astrological age of Taurus and was responsible for ushering in the new age of Aries, pledging to take his people to "the Promised Land," which was the "Kingdom of Light"—an inner kingdom. It was said that "the light shineth in the darkness: but the darkness comprehended it not."[42]

This biblical passage could refer to an initiatory process, which was identified with light and enlightenment. The objective of all initiation ceremonies was to enable individuals to see true beauty and gain a knowledge of truth.[43] Unfortunately, during Moses' time, as had happened before, the teachings were soon dogmatized and their potency destroyed. The seed planted within the chosen people did not continue to develop, and thus the opportunity for a lasting connection to divinity was soon lost.

It may be appropriate to view this as the last attempt by the Elohim to directly intervene in human development by manipulating the human lineage or form in the physical realm. There may have been no other special endowments of one race or tribe. However, it was by no means their last effort at awakening the physical form to its inherent function as a vehicle of light. Instead, the seed may have been planted in all of humanity. And the Elohim undoubtedly did not abandon their seedbeds but continued to nurture the seeds more indirectly as world teachers.

The Great Gardeners—Our World Teachers

Through the eons the Elohim sent numerous world teachers to Earth to awaken and to aid people in their attainment of higher spiritual consciousness. Thus, it is said that when the great Wiraccocha came to the Andes after the great flood, he brought people the light. He helped early Andean people emerge from a long period of darkness that had fallen on their world after the collapse of the preceding ancient civilization. From this perspective, the Inca were the last remnants of a particular early seed-ing of light.

It is likely that, throughout history, the Elohim have come down to Earth in physical form to tend to their seedbeds. One of the greatest world teachers came long before the time of Wiraccocha in the form of the great Egyptian known as Tehuti, or Thoth—later called Hermes Trismegistus by the Greeks.[44] The legendary Hermes brought his people many gifts including the arts, mathematics, astronomy, astrology, and all types of healing.

However, his primary gift was the doctrine of inner light and the teaching of Osirus. Hermes taught that light was universal and that light, which was God, dwelt in the heart of every man. He had the early Egyp-tians repeat, "I am the Light," and he spoke about the true nature of light.

> ...*Light is the true man, although men may not recognize it,*
> *although they neglect it. Osirus is the Light, He came forth from*
> *the Light, He dwells in the Light, He is the Light, The Light is*
> *hidden everywhere; it is in every rock and in every stone. When a*
> *man becomes one with Osirus the Light, then he becomes one with*
> *the whole of which he was a part, then he can see the Light in*
> *everyone, however thickly veiled: All the rest is not; but the Light is.*
> *The Light is the life of men. To every man—though there are*
> *glorious ceremonies, though there are many duties for the priest*
> *to do, and many ways in which he should help men—that Light is*
> *nearer than aught else, within his very heart. For every man the*
> *Reality is nearer than any ceremony, and ceremonies should not be*
> *done away with, for I have not come to destroy but to fulfill. When*
> *a man knows, he goes beyond the ceremony, he goes to Osirus, he*
> *goes to the Light, the Light Amen-Ra from which all came forth,*
> *to which all shall return.*[45]

To the pharaoh Hermes he gave the motto: "Look for the Light." He taught the pharaoh that only a king who had light in his heart could rule well. To the people, Hermes gave the motto: "Thou art the Light. Let that Light shine." And the people learned to say of their dead, "They have gone to the Light." Finally, to the priests, Hermes gave secret instructions that became part of the great mystery teachings.

Great leaders and teachers who were believed by their followers to be god-men also came to the Toltec and the Zapotec people of Central America, who were allegedly of the same remnant seed (descendants of god-seeds planted in ancient times). Quetzalcoatl and Pacal Votan are two of the extraordinary figures found in the myths and historical records of this region. Although we know little about them, judging by their cultural legacy, their teachings must have been profound. One tale of early Toltec origin is the story of the Smokey Mirror, as retold here by contemporary *nagual* don Miguel Ruiz. Tezcatlipoca, the Smokey Mirror, was an aspect of Quetzalcoatl. In later times, Tezcatlipoca represented the world of darkness and Quetzalcoatl represented the world of light. The following is an old version of the story from the time before their polarization:

> *One night the Smokey Mirror had a dream, in a cave deep under the great Pyramid of the Sun at the sacred site we know as Teotihuacán. And in this dream the Smokey Mirror traveled far up and through the great pyramid and far out into the night sky into the world of the stars and shining, swirling galaxies. He looked up and around at the stars, and he saw that they were made of light. He looked up into the space between the stars, and he saw that it was made of light. Then he looked down at his hands and saw that they, too, were made of stars and that the stars were made of light. And he looked at the space between the stars that were his hands, and he saw that they were made of light. And in that moment the Smokey Mirror awakened forever from the dream of darkness, the dream of this planet. He saw that we are nothing but Light. He saw that everything is made of light and that the light from deep within the universe brings us knowledge of who we really are. The Smokey Mirror discovered that we all are the children of light.*

Quetzalcoatl, the legendary plumed serpent known as Reed One, born about A.D. 1000, is said to have revitalized Teotihuacán, the great ceremonial complex abandoned by the Teotihuacános centuries before, as well as Chichén Itzá, an ancient Mayan city in central Yucatán, and, perhaps most importantly, the spiritual vision of the people of Mesoamerica. With many of the great ceremonial centers abandoned around A.D. 650, much of the spiritual vitality of Mesoamerica was lost or distorted. Until the time of

Quetzalcoatl, the ancient teachings were largely forgotten. Quetzalcoatl brought the last spiritual impulse to the people of Mesoamerica before their worldview was swept under by Aztec and later Spanish conquests.

Philosopher and author Edmond Bordeaux Szekely believes that Quetzalcoatl was considered the catalyst of light itself, the force that produced germination of the seed and a more abundant life. He was the Osirus of Mesoamerica. Moreover, according to Szekely, Quetzalcoatl was a symbol of the union of polarities. Depicted as the serpent with the wings of a bird, he represented the essence of the struggle toward the light. If man can overcome gravity, the force that pulls his attention into the confines of the material world, he can become like Quetzalcoatl, who represents light in physical form yet freed from the confines of matter.[46]

Some researchers, such as Laurette Sejourne, a Mexican archaeologist, believe that the legendary Tula, the home of Quetzalcoatl, was actually Teotihuacán. The ruins of Tula, north of Mexico City, are thought to have been built and inhabited much later by the Aztec.[47]

Teotihuacán, located just northeast of Mexico City, was built by the Teotihuacános, people believed to have been preceded by the Olmec. The great complex of Teotihuacán, which means "the place where man becomes God," is perhaps the most spectacular ancient ruin in Mesoamerica. The present site includes the massive Pyramid of the Sun and the Pyramid of the Moon. Originally the city of Teotihaucán extended over 12 miles and was the largest city in the world, with as many as 200,000 inhabitants.[48] By most accounts, it was built at least 100 years before the birth of Christ. Although no one knows where the Teotihuacános came from, it is well documented that Teotihuacán was a huge and extraordinary ceremonial center. The entire ceremonial complex was an initiation chamber designed to connect the people, the children of light, to their origins.

American engineer Hugh Harleston, Jr. established that the design of Teotihaucán presupposed a complex understanding of the solar system, including extensive mathematical, astronomical, and cosmic data.[49] Harleston found that the geometry of the Pyramid of the Sun functioned as a clock based on the equinoxes. Further, researchers verified that the west face of the Pyramid of the Sun and all the city streets were oriented to the setting of the Pleiades.[50] Clearly whoever built the structure was aware of advanced and comprehensive astronomical and geodetic data.

Moreover, Harleston discovered evidence that the citadel was a calendric device that demonstrated the precise orbits of all known planets.[51]

Perhaps even more astonishing, Harleston found evidence that the builders of Teotihuacán had knowledge of the speed of light in addition to other advanced mathematical concepts. Mathematically, what he deduced from the design of the citadel walls and structure was so complex and exact that he felt the resulting architecture could only have been produced by a sophisticated computer.[52] The fact that ancients could have had such knowledge is in itself extraordinary.

In his book *The Mysteries of the Mexican Pyramids,* Peter Thompkins speculates that the builders of Teotihuacán had to be operating from some higher state of consciousness that allowed them the benefit of more cosmic and therefore simpler mathematics through which they could establish relationships, including the basic constants of our three-dimensional math.[53] Further, he suggests that the pyramid complex was "intended to hint to latecomers to expand their consciousness for a clearer view of the cosmos and of man's relation to the whole."[54] Thus from the viewpoint of current thought, it seems likely that the Teotihuacán complex was a great cosmic blueprint to be used as an initiation center for the children of light—both past, present, and future incarnations. The design and function of the entire complex in both its design and function demonstrates advanced esoteric knowledge long lost to humanity. The last people of Mesoamerica to fathom such mysteries were the Toltecs, who under the tutelage of Quetzalcoatl spiritually enlivened much of Mesoamerica before their vision was also lost to history.

In the East, other great teachers came to India and Tibet to tell the story of the light—including Krishna, the Hindu deity worshiped as the eighth incarnation of Vishu (who is associated with the sun), and Buddha. Approximately 2,600 years ago, Buddha, known in various manifestations as "the illuminated one," "the illuminator," and "Infinite Light," taught the path to enlightenment.

Then some 2,000 years ago, a human god-seed and great teacher from the Hebrew tribe known as Jesus also pursued his mission to show humankind the path of light:

> *"I am the light of the world, he who follows me shall not walk in darkness, but shall find for himself the light of life."* **John 8:12**

"He who believes in me has already seen him who sent me. I have come into this world as light, so that whoever believes in me may not remain in darkness." **John 12:46**

"For previously you were ignorant, but now you have been enlightened by our Lord, and you should therefore live as children of light." **Paul to the Ephesians 5:8**

About 600 years after Jesus's life on Earth, another great teacher of light, Mohammed, came to tend the garden. In the land of the Islam, Mohammed was considered a mirror of the divine, as demonstrated in the following passage written about him:

> *God is the light*
> *Of the heavens and the earth.*
> *The parable of His Light*
> *Is as if there were a Niche*
> *And within it a Lamp:*
> *The Lamp enclosed in Glass:*
> *The glass as it were*
> *A brilliant star:*
> *Lit from a blessed Tree,*
> *An Olive, neither of the East*
> *Nor of the West*
> *Whose Oil is well-nigh*
> *Luminous,*
> *Though fire scarce touched it:*
> *Light upon Light!*
> *God doth guide*
> *Whom He will*
> *To His Light.*[55]

These great world teachers were, like those before them from many traditions and cultures, great Elohim who came in human form to serve as examples for all people and to prepare the remnant seed for future enlightenment.

Now, some 2,600 years later and about 500 years since Wayu's time, humanity stands at the threshold of a new collective awakening. As the cosmic cycles of time are telling us, it is the time for a major turn upon the spiral path of evolving human consciousness, when the light that has descended into matter begins the ascent back to its origin, the light. The great teachers have shown the way to higher consciousness. Now it is essential for all children of light to find their own inner light. This is the key to all the great mysteries.

We are and always have been god-seeds, enacting the drama of an evolutionary process that will ultimately lead us to full divinity. That the mystery teachings have endured for so long lends credence to this viewpoint. It is time for humanity to awaken the light-codes deep within each person, to attain higher consciousness and a greater understanding of our role in the universe.

3

MAYAN AND INCAN SEEDBEDS

W E DO NOT KNOW WHO THE ANCIENT PEOPLES OF Mesoamerica and Peru were or where they came from. The records they left, including glyphs carved in stone tablets, pottery fragments, and ruins of megalithic structures remain mysterious. There is no intact cultural history. Their legends have been distorted by sixteenth-century clerics. However, even the most cursory of study indicates there was something extraordinary about the Olmec, Zapotec, Teotihuacáno, Maya, Tiahuanaco, and Inca people. Undoubtedly, they knew where they came from and why they were here.

Because the records of these early cultures are sketchy, and interpretations of their worldviews have been limited and culturally biased, our perspective of these cultures is necessarily subjective. However, the following is an attempt to depict the worldview of these ancient peoples in order to further understand what was lost when these cultures were ravaged and disappeared.

World-ages of the Ancients
The cultures that flourished throughout Mesoamerica and ancient Peru declined well before the advent of written historical records. They were

thriving seedbeds of consciousness, carefully tended by the Elohim, the great god-men of the mythological past.

This does not mean that viewed from the twentieth-century these cultures were without problems. They embodied injustices and social inequities found throughout the world. Even in the best light some of their social practices—which included human sacrifice—seem bizarre to us, while in the worst light they appear barbarous. Although we may never fully understand these cultures, it is clear that they had something we have lost.

An important concept to the Inca, Maya, and Aztec people was the notion of world-ages. This idea is important for both understanding the worldviews of these cultures and for deciphering the symbolism of their myths.

The Incan notion of world-ages was first expressed in writing in 1584 by Felipe Guaman Poma de Ayala, a nobleman living in Peru. He wrote a letter to King Philip II of Spain encouraging him to adopt a more lenient policy toward the people of Peru on the grounds that they were quite civilized, no doubt had been for some time, and thus should not be treated barbarously by the Spaniards. The king, however, was not moved.[1]

In this letter, Poma de Ayala described the Incan concept of the five world-ages. According to his account, in the first age, people lived in caves, contended with wild animals, and "wandered lost in an unknown land, leading a nomadic life." In the second age, the people lived in crude round houses, broke "virgin earth," and lived in settlements. In the third age, which was a golden age, the people lived in houses like those of his day, had marriage customs, developed complex agriculture, shared a tradition of emergence from sacred springs and caves, and most importantly, lived harmoniously together. There was no conflict in their world until the fourth age, which was known as the Age of the Warriors—a time of armed conflict. Lastly, the fifth age was the period of the great Inca empire, which continued through the time of the Spanish conquest. Interestingly, the term "sun" is used interchangeably with the concept of world-age. Thus, the Inca empire arose during the time of the fifth sun or fifth world-age.

In the contemporary world, there is a tendency to think that reality as we perceive it is essentially unchanging. By contrast, the indigenous cultures of Mesoamerica and Peru understood that reality was dynamic. They marked the birth of a new reality, or worldview, with the advent of a new sun, which brought renewed vitality and ultimately a new cultural reality. It may be factually true that each prior age, or "sun," was destroyed due to some physical catastrophe and that the following age was born out of the resultant chaos. Or it may be that the catastrophe causing a new age was primarily psychological in nature, such as the emotional trauma resulting from massive cultural upheaval. In any case, the floods of great and rapid change washed away all but residual memory of prior ages.

The Spanish priest and chronicler, Mart'n de Murea also wrote about the Incan concept of the five suns:

> *Since the creation of the world until this time there have passed*
> *four suns without [counting] the one which presently illuminates us.*
> *The first was lost by water, the second by the falling of the sky on the*
> *earth… the third sun they say failed by fire. The fourth by air.*
> *They take this fifth sun greatly into account and have it painted*
> *and symbolized in the temple Curicancha [the Inca Temple of the*
> *Sun in Cuzco] and placed in their* quipus *until the year 1554.[2]*

The Concept of Space/Time Reality

To truly understand the idea of a world-age from the perspective of the Inca, it is necessary to grasp how their ancestors viewed physical reality. First, their concept of reality was multi-tiered. The Inca used the term "this space/time" when referring to the reality we normally perceive in three dimensions through our five senses. They did not limit their perception to the linear time that defines our basic reality; they understood that there were other realities and that this space/time was relative to perspective. Many years after the Incan empire collapsed, Albert Einstein proved that this space/time was indeed relative. Although the term space/time continuum is associated with Einstein, it was also understood by the Inca.

Those among the Inca and other indigenous cultures who mastered these broader perceptual abilities were able to function in multiple dimensions. They developed these capacities through the rigors of training and spiritual initiations. Although we cannot now entirely comprehend such multifaceted perceptual abilities, these skills were not lost entirely but have been preserved in *nagual*, shamanic, and mystical traditions. Moreover, such higher capacities exist in all of us, whether we perceive them or not.

The Inca believed that each new world-age shifted the perception of space/time and linear reality. That is why the great Pachacuti Inca, the ninth Inca leader, was said to have overturned space and time. He not only built the Inca empire, he brought forth a new perception of the world, initiating the fifth sun, or the fifth world-age.

It has been said that the light of the sun carries higher knowledge, which is perhaps the basis for its worldwide worship. The belief throughout Mesoamerica and Peru that each new world-age was inaugurated by a new sun supports this idea. When the light of a new sun shone upon the world, it brought with it new potential and new knowledge.

The Maya and the Aztec also incorporated similar concepts of suns, or world-ages into their worldview. The Aztec believed that there had been four previous world-ages and that their culture came to prominence in the fifth age, documented by the famous Aztec stone calendar. Arranged around the sun god, Tonatiuh, are symbols of four ages, which also appear in manuscripts such as *Leyenda de los Soles*, the *Chimalpopoc Codex*, and the *Cuauhtitlan Annals*. These accounts describe time cycles of 52 years, the Aztec centuries.

Mayan Time Line

The Mayan world, which once covered the eastern half of Mesoamerica, included all of present-day Guatemala, Belize, the Yucatán Peninsula, western Honduras, El Salvador, most of Mexico east of the isthmus at Tehuntepec, and most of Chiapas. Like the Aztec, the Maya believed there were multiple creations and that each was marked by a different sun. However, the Maya marked time with four, not five, ages. The Mayan calendar documents the commencement of the current age as between August 6 and August 13, 3113 B.C. This age, according to the calendar, is scheduled to end on A.D. December 21, 2012.

In his book *The Mayan Factor*, historian and visionary José Argüelles presents a helpful historical time line based on the Mayan calendar, beginning in 3113 B.C.[3] Around the commencement of the current world-age, as measured by the Mayan calendar, Stonehenge was built, and shortly thereafter the Great Pyramid of Egypt was constructed. This age began in the approximate time period that corn (maize) became widely cultivated in North America.

The Maya were relative latecomers to Mesoamerica. The first great culture in the region was that of the Olmec, who appeared on the Gulf of Mexico by 2000 B.C.—possibly earlier. Although no one knows where they came from or where they went, they left behind giant, beautifully carved heads; artwork that depicted tall, bearded, nonindigenous god-men; and many yet unexcavated ruins. While the mysterious Mayan culture thrived in Mesoamerica, the Vedic culture began in India, Moses led his people from Egypt, and the Chavin culture emerged in the Andes.

About 600 B.C., the Zapotec appeared in Oaxaca, where they founded a spectacular ceremonial center known as Monte Albán. These early people left behind stunning sculptures known as the *danzantes*, or the dancers. They are marked with signs from the Mayan calendar, which date them to 600 B.C. By this time, in the lowlands, the early Maya had begun to erect mountain pyramids. Roughly in this time period, Buddha, Lao-tzu, the Upanishads, and Confucius made their appearance in the East. Then Western civilization as we have come to perceive it began to flourish, for it was during this period that Socrates, Aristotle, and Plato set forth their philosophies.

Around the year 200 B.C., to the north of Monte Albán, the Teotihaucáno began to build Teotihuacán—the largest and one of the most spectacular ceremonial centers in Mesoamerica. In the high plateaus of the Andes, a new civilization took form, transforming the landscape with vertical archipelagos and embodying a divinely inspired worldview. In the Mayan world, monumental structures and artwork began to appear. By the time Teotihuacán was completed around A.D. 300, the Gnostics were spreading the teachings of Christ, Tiahuanaco was flourishing, and strange lines appeared upon the Nazca plains. The influence of Teotihuacán began to spread south, and the classical period of the Maya was well under way.

A New View of the Classical Maya

The classical period of the Maya lasted until about A.D. 830, leaving a legacy of amazing architectural and artistic achievements like Tikal, Copán, and Palenque. At the end of the classical period, these spectacular sites were mysteriously abandoned and destroyed. To the north, the Teotihuacáno also had vanished, as had the Olmec long before, leaving Teotihuacán and Monte Albán empty. To the south, Tiahuanaco, the great civilization of the high Andes of Peru, lay in ruin after the Tiahuanaco disappeared.

About A.D. 1000 the Toltec emerged near present-day Mexico City and reclaimed Teotihuacán. The year A.D. 947 marked the birth of One Reed, the legendary Quetzalcoatl, known by his southern brothers as Kukulkan. Then the warrior clans rose and overpowered the Peruvian Andes. The Middle East and Europe were ravished by the Crusades. The Dark Ages were underway.

Argüelles has written extensively about the Maya and their sacred calendar in *The Mayan Factor*, which was the impetus for the Harmonic Convergence in 1987 and gave rise to new views fundamental to our understanding of the age we are now entering. In his book, Argüelles describes how the Mayan calendar functioned. Briefly, the present cycle, which began in 3113 B.C. and will end in A.D. 2012, consists of 5,125 solar years (equal to 1,872,000 days). A 52-year period is central to the Mayan system as it was to the later Aztec calendar. Their 5,200-year cycle can be broken into 260 units of 20 *tun*, each of which is called a *katun*, or 13 units of 400 *tun*, each of which are called *baktun*. The Mayan calendar of the world-age in which we currently live has 20 *baktun*, each of which lasts about 394 solar years.

Several of these *baktun* are of special interest. The first *baktun* of this world-age, Baktun 0, occurred between 3113 and 2718 B.C., and it is called the Baktun of the Star Planting. According to Argüelles, this was the time of the planting of star transmission—a time of the seeding of the light of consciousness on this planet. Baktun 11, the period preceding the present *baktun*, which began in 1224 and ended in 1618, is called the Baktun of the Hidden Seed. This was the time of the conquest of the Inca and Aztec empires, and also the time of the Cartesian split, when mechanical explanations of physical and biological phenomena came into prominence, and the sacred worldview was lost. Mind became divided from matter; the mechanical replaced the sacred. The Dark Ages descended, and the human seed fell deep into the realm of material darkness. Baktun 12, called the Baktun of Transformation of Matter, includes our present time and is scheduled to end on December 21, 2012, the date the Mayan calendar ends.

While little is known about the culture of the classical Maya, the culture of the postclassical Maya is well documented. All of the pre-Hispanic screenfold books date from the late postclassical period (A.D. 1250–1541). Numerous colonial works written by both Spanish and native scholars provide information on this later period, including the well-known *Popol Vuh*, which is considered the oldest documented mythology of the New World. Written in the colonial period by a 16th-century Quich'e Maya, it was actually inspired by older sources.

Recently, a new breed of archaeologists and ethnographers, like Dennis and Barbara Tedlock, have set aside their cultural bias and opened doorways to the Maya worldview. They are also adding to our knowledge of the culture of the classical Maya, who are considered the apex of their civilization. In addition, researchers such as David Freidel and his colleagues Linda Schele and Joy Parker, the authors of *Maya Cosmos*, are helping us to see through the eyes of the Maya.

Freidel and his colleagues began their work by first respecting the shamanic worldview of the Maya, rather than disregarding it because it did not fit their own cultural preconceptions. As a result, they found that the study of current rituals could shed considerable light on prior mysteries. They also found that fragments of art and architecture from the classical Mayan period provided access to an ancient cosmology. In this manner, they discovered that the Mayan ruins and artwork contained symbols of the Mayan view of the world's creation and were literally maps of the sky at the moment of creation. Moreover, they came to understand how the Mayan ruins were designed and used as instruments for accessing spiritual power. Such perspectives allow us to gain a fundamental understanding of who these people were, where they thought they came from, and why they believed they were here.

Modern archaeoastronomy, a study of ancient astronomy, has been used by Freidel and his colleagues to examine Mayan ruins and the structure of their myths with astonishing results. By looking back at the progression of stars in the sky on critical dates, researchers have been able to understand the cosmic symbolism that is central to many ancient myths and legends. Not only does this astronomical information often tell us the date of certain myths, it deciphers the code of the mythic language. Moreover, observation of equinoxes and solstices has revealed the significance and the particular alignment of certain sacred sites. When Freidel and his colleagues studied the night sky as it appeared during the Mayan creation period, they made some exciting discoveries. But first, lets look at the corresponding mythology.

Although no one knows the name of the Mayan mother goddess of the classical period, Freidel and his colleagues refer to her as the First Mother and to her husband as the First Father, or the Maize God. He was the divine being who oversaw the creation of the new cosmos on August 13, 3113 B.C. (based on our current Julian calendar, September 20, 3113 B.C., the autumnal equinox).

There is no manuscript that tells the creation story of the classical Maya, but it was encoded into their monuments. At Quirigua, in Guatemala, a series of stelae were found that are key references.

The Mayan creation story is also told in the postclassical *Popol Vuh*, which relates that the First Father was the creator who raised up the "sky tree," which is a symbol of the Milky Way (Wakan-Chan as the Maya called it). Before that time, the sky was still lying down, and there was no light. The First Father, was killed in Xibalba (the underworld) by the Lords of Death. His sons, the twins, went to the underworld, defeated his killers, and brought their father back to life. Artwork from the Mayan classical period portrays the creation myth and shows the Maize God reborn through a cracked turtle shell. The stelae refer to these images and to the setting of "the three stones of creation." The three stones have been identified as the three stars in the belt of Orion. Dennis Tedlock has observed that the contemporary Maya place three stones in the center of their hearth,[4] a ritual that connects their life in this space/time to the time of creation.

In Mayan mythology, the Milky Way is portrayed as a crocodile, the "cosmic monster," a canoe, and the tree of life. The turtle shell from which the Maize God is reborn is often linked with the constellation of Orion. Other representations found in artwork related to the creation story show the constellation Gemini, the twins. These sources identify the place of creation as the part of the sky where Orion and Gemini are found.[5]

The image of the double-headed serpent, also portrayed in Mayan artwork, is often found draped around the tree of life or the Milky Way. It is believed to be a representation of the ecliptic, the line of constellations in which the sun rises and sets each year. The serpent was also a symbol of what is known as the cosmic umbilicus, the line of energy that connects each human god-seed with its celestial origin. Freidel has said that to the Maya, these serpents were symbols of the path along which supernaturals traveled on their way to being manifested in this world. The Maize God was portrayed as being reborn from the serpent's mouth. Freidel also points out that according to the Palace Tablet, found in Palenque, a ruin of a Mayan city in what is now the Mexican state of Chiapas, human souls find new bodies by traveling along the serpent's gullet.[6]

In Tikal a series of bones were found that have scenes carved into them showing the creator god and two paddlers (the twins) in the sky riding through the Milky Way to where they set the three stones into the hearth of Orion. Linda Schele explains these carvings as follows:

> *I realized that the Paddlers bring the Maize God to the place of the three stones of Creation and to the turtle shell, which is Orion so that he can be reborn and create a new universe. He is the Wak-Chan-Ahaw who makes everything happen.*

> *Two painted pots [found elsewhere] depicting this same canoe scene confirm its association with the myth of the First Father as the Maize God. One has a black background showing that the action occurs at a lightless time before the First Father raised the sky. The narrative scene includes three episodes from the story. In one the Jaguar and Stingray Paddlers (the twins) paddle a canoe carrying the Maize God to the place of creation. He carries a seed bag on his chest so that he can plant the seeds that are the Pleiades when he raises the Wakan-Chan or as Enrique Florescano suggested to us, so that he can use them to form the flesh of human beings after creation is done. Below the canoe the reclining figure of the Maize God emerges from the mouth of the Vision Serpent in a position that mimics exactly the emergence of a child from his mother's birth canal."[7]*

When Freidel and Schele put a series of symbols together with a map of the sky as it was at sunset August 13, 3113 B.C., the date of the beginning of the current Mayan world-age, they found it was an exact representation of the myth. Moreover, they found that in a great cosmic drama, the sky, in this model, replays the creation story in the progression of stars. As the night proceeds, the crocodile (the Milky Way) transforms into a canoe running east to west. The two paddlers propel Itzam, the creator (the Maize God), to the place of creation between Orion and Gemini. There the three stones of creation that make up the belt of Orion are set in place. The Maize God is reborn from Orion, and his umbilicus stretches out to become the ecliptic. On the day of the creation of the current world-age, the map of the night sky reflects the following story: At sunset Orion is still in the center of the sky. As it sinks to the western horizon, it takes with it a handful of seeds (the Pleiades) to be planted in the earth. The Pleiades were called "a handful of maize seeds" by the Maya.[8]

Such discoveries pose important and perplexing questions about the knowledge of the ancient Maya. Could they have known about esoteric teachings of the Adam Kadmon and the new spiritual human? Could they have known that according to these teachings the human spiritual seed came from the Pleiades and that the Elohim, the god-men, came from the great Orion gateway? Or did the creators themselves paint the story of creation across the sky that was later encoded in the ancient language of myth itself?

Mayan Remnants of Light Seeding

Because artwork and great monuments of the Mayan classical period recreate the map of the sky at the time of creation, they seem to suggest that the Maya came from the stars. In addition, because of their design and through the use of the principles of sacred geometry, these artworks and monuments held open gateways to higher consciousness and the divine. The ancient Maya used their elaborate ceremonial centers to reconnect with their cosmic origin and to be spiritually revitalized.

It is well established that the Maya of the classical period inherited much of their worldview from the Olmec, who preceded them, including concepts that are the basis of their calendar and their sacred architecture. Researchers such as Freidel who have interpreted stelae found at the Olmec site in La Venta and analyzed the structure of the compound, have concluded that the complex "was built as an act of devotion" and to invoke sacred power.[9] They found that these structures were filled with precious stones, magical symbols, and power objects used by the Olmec to open energetic portals to other worlds. As Freidel states, the Olmec and the Maya did not build their massive structures using coercion but through the willing work and dedication of the people. Literally thousands of people, generation after generation, helped to create enormous stone edifices. They did so because these edifices acted as anchors to the divine, and also because access to the spiritual realm was vital to their existence.

According to Freidel and his colleagues, the Olmec and Maya conceived of their plazas as "watery places," or the primordial sea, where spiritual communication could occur: "Both saw plazas as places where people could swim through the incense in the ecstasy of dance.... Plazas shimmered with the hidden currents of the Primordial Sea, stairways descended from the summits of Creation, mountains shaped paths between worlds."[10] Panels at Palenque show a "dance of rebirth" at a watery place, which is identified as a location in the supernatural world. Below this "watery place" are images of water lilies from which skeletal heads grow like seeds.[11] Kent Reilly, who has extensively studied the Olmec, has pointed out that flying figures and a sensation of swimming found in Olmec artwork indicate trance states and that other world cultures document trance states in a similar way. For example, tribesmen of the Kalahari, the desert region of South Africa, make swimming motions when they are in deep trance, and the Monte Albán ecstatic dancers include figures of swimmers.[12]

Sacred Sites as Gateways to Higher Consciousness

Virtually all the classical sites of Mesoamerica display the builders' use of sacred geometry and were built as portals to spiritual realms. The use of sacred correspondence was understood by the ancient people associated with these sites as a way to access divine energy. Evidence of sacred correspondence has been found at Palenque, Copán, Chichén Itzá, and many other sites. Many of these sites were also geographically aligned with the belt of Orion.[13]

Palenque, located in present-day Chiapas, is considered by many people to be one of the most spectacular ancient sites in Mesoamerica. The founder of Palenque was Pacal Votan. José Argüelles believes that the incarnation of Pacal Votan corresponds with a heightened spiritual impulse that reached the Mayan world between A.D. 631 and A.D. 683. Pacal's tomb is dated A.D. 683. According to legend, Pacal Votan was an avatar, a great master, and referred to himself as a "serpent, an initiate, a possessor of knowledge."[14] When Pacal died, his son built a series of three temples in his honor—known as the Temples of Inscriptions. These temples record and replicate the events of creation—the rebirth of the Maize God and the creation of humans from maize (the seed) and water.

As previously noted, "serpent" was the term reserved for very high initiates, individuals who understood the use of energy and harmonic vibration. There are references in Mayan history to the Brotherhood of the Serpent. Zamma, the creator god described above who was taken to the place of creation in a canoe and became the Maize God, is mentioned in the *Chilam Balam*. Zamma was said to be a "Great Serpent of the East." In this context the serpents may be viewed as members of the great extraterrestrial brotherhood of advanced beings dedicated to helping humanity evolve—otherwise known as Elohim.

Argüelles says that the legends about Pacal tell us he was sent from his homeland, known as Valum Chivim, to the Yucatán, the land of the Maya. He reputedly reached the Mayan world by going through an energetic gateway called the Kuxan Suum, or road to the sky, through what he called the "dwelling of the 13 serpents." The myth tells us Pacal founded Palenque when he arrived at Valum Votan on the Usuamacinta River.[15]

The sculpture found on Pacal's tomb, which was not discovered until 1952, seems to suggest that Pacal had an extraterrestrial origin. One of the most intriguing pieces of artwork from the Mayan classical period shows Pacal at death falling into the sky tree and entering what the Maya called the "white road," our Milky Way. Above him the sky tree soars with the double-headed serpent visible in its branches, indicating that he is undergoing a great transformation. Overall, the sculpture suggests that, like the legendary Christ, Pacal is transformed into divinity and escapes the illusion of mortality. Portrayed first as an avatar in physical form, he is later represented as a creator god.[16]

Argüelles believes that the Maya were star-beings, or time-lords, who had a specific mission here on Earth. He suggests that Valum Chivim is a starbase, possibly located in the Pleiades and implies that the Maya may have originated from an extraterrestrial source. Further, he argues that the "dwelling of the thirteen serpents" represents an intergalactic passageway to the high planes of energy beyond our solar system and explains that the Mayan term Kuxan Suum means "the road to the sky leading to the umbilical cord of the Universe."[17] This concept is similar to the luminous cord that connects the solar plexus to the sky referenced in *nagualism* and other shamanic systems. Argüelles further suggests that the place of the underworld, called Xibalba in the *Popol Vuh*, is a reference to the world of manifestation, this space/time. He states that the Maya saw this reality as a realm where we are tested by taking human form. Thus Xibalba is a representation of the world of illusion into which humans incarnate, a concept referred to in the *nagual* tradition as the dream of the planet.

Moreover, according to Argüelles, Pacal and the other masters of the Mayan classical period consciously left this world and returned to their home in the stars. He indicates that the nine lords that are symbolized on Pacal's crypt are nine masters (god-men) that preceded Pacal. Argüelles also states that the mythological figure personified in the human form of Quetzalcoatl/Kukulkan, who he says lived from A.D. 947 to A.D. 999, was an incarnation of Pacal.[18]

The classical Maya, the Zapotec, and the Teotihuacáno all existed at approximately the same time and all demonstrated a profound understanding of the universe. From what we can glean from the sites and other evidence they left behind, these cultures shared a purpose. They desired to replicate on the physical plane the glory of the higher worlds. They consciously reenacted the story of the emergence of the god-seed through their rituals, their art, and their architecture as a way of grounding their lives in this space/time.

The great kings, known by their subjects as god-men, oversaw the development of their ceremonial centers and sacred monuments. Although it is not essential to know where these god-men came from or where they went in order to comprehend the story of the spiritual human, it is necessary to understand some things about the sacred sites they left behind.

During this period, in Mesoamerica and Peru large numbers of people went through initiation ceremonies to experience the higher worlds. The sites associated with these cultures were used for initiation into the greater mysteries, and substantial resources were used in their construction. In the worldview of the people of these cultures, the ceremonial centers were vital, since they connected the people to their innate divinity.

In addition, these sites were used as massive stone timepieces to track the solstices and equinoxes; to track the movement of stars, planets, and various constellations; and to track much larger cycles of time that we cannot yet fully understand.

The most important function of these sites was to bring the Earth plane into a sacred correspondence with the higher worlds. Sacred correspondences created the possibility for direct interaction with the higher planes—a time when the three stones of creation (representing physical, mental, and spiritual forces at work on the Earth) could be aligned. One of the first acts of the creator god was to place the three stones of creation in the firmament. As previously noted, contemporary Maya still place three stones on their hearths. Such correspondences represent a human avenue to divinity.

Archaeoastronomy and the Mayan Prophecies for a New World

The study of archaeoastronomy has added significantly to our understanding of the Maya. A short review of a few concepts related to Earth's celestial movement will assist in perceiving the worldview of the Maya and the Inca, both of whom also called themselves the children of the sun and both of whom had a well-developed cosmology.

We know that in the Northern Hemisphere on the summer solstice the sun rises and sets at its most northerly point—making the June solstice the longest day. On the winter solstice, the sun rises and sets at its most southerly point, making the December solstice the shortest day. We also know Earth's axis tilts relative to the sun—in each hemisphere tilting toward the sun in the summer and away from it in the winter. In March and September at the equinoxes, when day and night are equal, the tilt of Earth's axis relative to the sun is more sideways.

It may seem as if our sun orbits Earth every day, although we know it does not; rather it is the Earth's orbit that makes the sun appear to rise and set. The Earth moves around the sun in a fixed plane, and the sun also appears to move around the Earth. Over a year's time we see the sun move through the ecliptic, passing through the signs of the Zodiac. The tilt of Earth's axis also varies a bit in relation to the ecliptic. Even though these changes are slow, it is necessary to take them into account to determine where the sun may have risen at an ancient site or where it may rise in the future.

There is, in addition, an important concept that alters how we view the stars throughout history. Earth's axis actually wobbles slowly over 25,800 years, causing the planet to change its orientation to fixed stars. This movement, called precession, makes it appear as though the sun passes through different constellations. For the past 2000 years the sun has been rising in Pisces. It will soon rise in Aquarius. This phenomenon primarily affects stellar alignments at sites and is important in the study of archaeoastronomy, since stellar alignments are critical to marking the precise times of the solstices and equinoxes. For example, due to the effect of precession, the rise of the Pleiades changes by one degree every 72 years. Therefore, to determine what the night sky looked like in 3113 B.C., or the precise time of the solstice, it is necessary to take precession into account.

The complex phenomenon of precession was understood by both the Mayan and Incan shamans (*pag'os*) of Wayu's time. They were in charge of determining the exact times of solstices and had to refer to fixed stars like the Pleiades cluster because it was not possible to get such information from watching the sun. Due to precession the stellar alignments would vary. A knowledge of precession was also important in calibrating solar calendars.

It has been established that in ancient cultures all around the world, myths were used as symbolic language to maintain a record of the precession of the equinoxes and other celestial phenomenon. Further, as was established by historian Hertha von Dechend, a universal set of conventions was used worldwide to encrypt astronomical observations within myth.[19]

During the course of a precessional cycle, the equinox and solstice suns align with the Milky Way at certain times. In the 25,800-year cycle of precession there are alignments approximately every 6,400 years. The last alignment occurred in about 4400 B.C. when the fall equinox sun was in conjunction with the Milky Way. Dechend and Santillana indicate that this cosmic event coincided with the fabled prior golden age found in many myths. They state that after the golden age ended, humanity descended into a history of increasing disharmony.[20]

Now, some 6,400 years later, the next alignment of a solstice sun with the Milky Way is at hand. Author John Major Jenkins in his book *Maya Cosmogenesis 2012* points out that this particular conjunction of the December solstice sun and the Milky Way occurs at the end of one complete cycle of precession; that is, it only occurs every 25,800 years. According to Jenkins, this rare alignment coincides with the end of the current Mayan world-age (December 21, 2012) and the beginning of their new world-age, their fifth sun.[21]

If the last precessional cycle brought the seeding of human consciousness, it is interesting to consider what the Mayan prophecies for the beginning of their next world-age have to tell us. Jenkins theorizes that the Maya believed a full precessional cycle was related to the spiritual evolution of humanity, and that they saw the transitional period between world-ages as a tremendous opportunity for spiritual transformation and spiritual rebirth. The 2012 alignment occurs when the December solstice sun conjuncts the crossing point of the Milky Way in Sagittarius. An area in the sky called the dark rift—known to the Maya as the Xibalba bi, the road to the underworld—points right to this crossing point. The crossing point is found at the center of our galaxy, and the Maya called it the sacred tree. To them it indicated the place of creation.[22]

The ecliptic is the path followed by the sun and planets through the sky. It crosses through the Milky Way in two places—in the constellations of Gemini and Sagittarius—creating two opposite areas in the sky where a cross is formed by the intersection of the Milky Way and the ecliptic. The crossing point in Sagittarius appears to indicate the location of the galactic center. The Maya apparently knew this for they referred to this precise location as the center of creation, the cosmic womb. Jenkins suggests that when the solstice sun conjuncts the galactic center, a spiritual gateway will open.[23] Is it possible that this cosmic occurrence might catalyze a new leap in human potential?

Freidel's research, which draws on both myth and archaeoastronomy, has shown that the current Mayan world-age, which began in 3113 B.C., was portrayed in the night sky in the Gemini crossing point as a rebirth of the First Father. Jenkins explains that the 2012 calendar end date of the current Mayan world-age and the commencement of their new world-age, their fifth sun, symbolizes a cosmic rebirth of humanity.

As noted, on A.D. December 21, 2012 this center of the cosmos will conjunct with the solstice sun (metaphorically the First Father) in Sagittarius. Of course this rare alignment will not occur solely or precisely on A.D. December 21, 2012. The effects of this conjunction are already being felt and will be for the next 200 or so years. As Jenkins points out, there is no exact galactic center; the center is more like a field than a specific point, and it takes a while for our sun to move through this vast area. What is astrologically significant is that on A.D. December 21, 2012 the solstice sun will be three degrees from the galactic center.[24] Astrologically, a sun conjunction with a planet is a positive aspect indicating increased willpower and the unfolding of creative potential and initiative. However, the conjunction we are referring to is not with a planet; it is with our galaxy. One can only speculate on what the effect of a sun-galaxy conjunction will be.

There is another important conjunction that occurs at the end of the current Mayan world-age. Jenkins points out that the sun and the Pleiades conjunct on May 20, 2012, 60 days after the spring equinox. This will occur in the latitude of the Yucatán peninsula at the exact center of the sky, the zenith, and will be preceded by a solar eclipse. Jenkins cites evidence that the Mayan kings timed their accessions to power with sun-Pleiades conjunctions. It would appear that they believed Pleiades conjunctions[25] indicated a time of divine engendering. At the very least, the Maya understood that certain harmonious cosmic cycles could have positive counterparts on Earth.

There are many reasons why the equinoxes and solstices were important to ancient people, including determination of when to plant and harvest crops. Also, on a spiritual level it appears that our predecessors understood what some contemporary esotericists still believe—that the intervals before, during, and after the equinoxes and solstices are spiritually powerful times. It is said that these are the days when the higher planes of consciousness are more accessible. The Inca and their predecessors believed that when the solstice sun entered the Milky Way at dawn, the gateway to the higher worlds opened. To them, the idea of an opening between worlds was, as with the Maya of the classical period, far more than a metaphor.

There is another interesting belief associated with the precession of the equinoxes. It is an ancient esoteric concept that the precession of the equinoxes, which links the movement of the Earth and the movement of the sun, is related to the Pleiades. Esotericist J. J. Hurtak suggests that the Pleiades was considered to be the Mother Sun of our solar system, "the Sun beyond the Sun"—an old belief found in many cultures. Hurtak postulates that it takes 25,827.5 years for our solar system to revolve around the Pleiades.[26]

The concept of the Platonic Great Year, which is one full cycle of the precession of equinoxes, was also associated with the Pleiades. This may be because the Pleiades was used to track precession in many ancient cultures, including the cultures of Mesoamerica and Peru. It was also believed that there was a larger cosmic time cycle of which we are a part. Argüelles claims that this cycle of 25,800 years correlates to the four Mayan world-ages of 5,200 years each. This cycle he believes represents the period of human evolution on our planet, and that we are now in the last stage of that cycle.[27] In this context, it is interesting to note that according to the mythic records of the ancient civilizations of Lemuria and Atlantis, the first seedings of humanity occurred about 26,000 years ago at the beginning of the Platonic Great Year that is now ending.

There is, however, no scientific support for the premise that our solar system presently rotates around the Pleiades in a 25,827.5-year cycle, or at all. Based upon simple calculations it seems an unworkable premise. If our solar system did complete such an orbit in 25,827.5 years, it would have to do so at a rate of some 1,152,000 miles per hour, and that rate of speed presumably could be detected. We know that our sun and entire solar system are moving through space at the edge of the Milky Way at a very high speed that has been computed at 481,000 miles per hour.[28] Therefore, it is likely that the notion of an orbit around the Pleiades is only metaphoric.

Another interesting idea related to the Pleiades, called the photon belt theory, may also be metaphoric. According to this theory, which is popular in the New Age community, Earth is now being affected by a belt of high-frequency light particles that comes from the Pleiades. But this theory has not been scientifically accepted, and most scientists consider it a hoax.

It is also possible that such ideas are simply incompatible with the current scientific paradigm. At some later time we may be able to perceive other levels of reality, including those that exist outside of linear time. There may indeed be types of energy so subtle we cannot perceive them, and cycles of nonlinear time that we cannot presently measure.

Westerners are generally so enamored with the rational mind that they are often unwilling to consider other valid viewpoints. We have been stuck in Wayu's black box for a long, long time, but we are now beginning to emerge. Some people believe that our limited cultural lens has elevated science to a religion. As a culture, we are slowly relearning that scientific verification, limited as it often is, is not the sole basis for understanding the miraculous nature of life. The worldview of the ancients was not as perceptually limited as our own. Apparently, they understood far more about subtle phenomena than we do, an example being the concept of sacred correspondence (the reflection of sacred content in physical form here on Earth).

Inca Cosmic Vision and Divine Mirroring

The Inca were preceded by the Tiahuanaco, about whom very little is known. Within the Inca conception of world-ages, the Tiahuanaco period, which began about 200 B.C. and ended about A.D. 650, was considered a golden age. This was the time that preceded the age of the warriors, the period called the third sun, or third world-age.

The fourth age, or fourth sun, was the age of armed conflict within the Inca world. This was the time when the teachings of the creator god Wiraccocha were disregarded, and a warrior class emerged.

The fifth age was declared by Pachacuti, the ninth Inca ruler, who built the Inca empire. Under his direction the teachings of Wiraccocha became prominent again, and the Incan world once more reflected the laws of sacred correspondence.

Nowhere is the concept of sacred correspondence more evident than the spectacular Sacred Valley of the Inca, which is approximately 60 miles long and stretches from Pisac to Machu Picchu. Through the valley winds the beautiful Vilcanota (Urubamba) River, known in ancient times as the Sacred River. The ancients associated the river with the Mayu, their name for the Milky Way.

The Sacred Valley of the Incas: Myths and Symbols, by Fernando E. Elorrieta Salazar and Edgar Elorrieta Salazar, is a wonderful book that tells the history of the Andean people through their myths, symbols, and descriptions of their ritual spaces in a way that brings to life the essence of their spectacular cosmic vision. As the authors state, Inca myths were intended to legitimize the truth of what the Inca believed was their divine origin, as well as the superiority of Inca models of social, political, and religious organization. Thus the Inca materialized their ideal through myths and also by using the principles of sacred geometry to build structures that demonstrated a direct connection to their mythic reality.

Ancient peoples of Mesoamerica and Peru believed that everything was sacred and that a primary purpose of creation was to reflect divinity. From this viewpoint, physical creation existed to reflect in physical form that which is found at higher energetic levels. This concept of sacred correspondence was recognized by ancient thinkers worldwide. The Gnostics and the Greek, Hindu, Buddhist, Sufi, and Medieval Jewish philosophers all embraced the macrocosm-microcosm principle.[29] Medieval alchemists used the phrase "as above, so below" in referring to this idea. It is also the basis of the hologram. For the Inca, the Mayu or Milky Way was an axis for orientation and a reference map of the sky in which important constellations were located. They believed that certain constellations were important in creating abundance and well-being on Earth. Therefore, they built massive sacred structures representing the main constellations found in the Mayu, reinforcing their belief that the Sacred Valley and its river were a reflection of the Milky Way.

To Andean people, the sacred condor was considered the messenger of the divine. They also believed the condor carried the life force of those who died to the superior world and protected the spirits of ancestors. In Pisac, the city where the Sacred Valley begins, the Inca built a huge ritual space in the shape of a giant condor into a mountain. Because of its design, which is intentionally subtle as if to hide the majestic edifice from profane eyes, it appears to be flying over the thousands of tombs built into the cliffs. Moreover, there is also a constellation found in the Milky Way that the Inca called the condor.

The sacred tree was another important concept to the Andean people. The Quechua word for tree, *mallqui,* also means ancestor. Ancestors were considered protectors and mediators between the people, the forces of Earth, and the gods. In addition, the Inca believed certain trees were oracles. There is a constellation that they called Ali Pakita, the "split tree, or tree that has let fall part of itself," a form they recreated on Earth near the town of Ollantaytambo on the Patacancha River. Made of terraces and irrigation canals and used to grow sacred grains, corn, and quinoa, this massive 1,200-acre earth form is shaped like a tree with many roots. It has a wide trunk and branches that appear to hold rich fruit. The river flows through its middle like living sap, and the canals converge into two channels—one to irrigate the masculine aspect and one to irrigate the feminine aspect. The crown of the tree was designed to catch and reflect the light at sunset on the solstices.

The fruit of the tree, representing the seed of divinity itself, is the Pyramid of Pacaritanpu. According to legends, the great Inca themselves emerged through the windows of the Pyramid of Pacaritanpu, which were called the *paqarinas,* places of emergence from other dimensions. Thus, the Inca can be seen as the seeds within the fruit of the tree. In many cultures, the three worlds of sky, earth, and underworld were depicted as a world tree. For the Maya the world tree, or sky tree, was also a representation of the Milky Way from which all life arose.

According to the Inca myth of creation, Wiraccocha ordered the sun, moon, and stars to rise in the sky above Lake Titicaca so that there would be light in the world. He then created the descendants of the Inca, who came out of Lake Titicaca and followed the sacred river, until they came to a beautiful valley. There they entered the "basement" of a building known as the "house of dawn," or the Pacaritanpu, which was aligned with the first light of the solstice and was the mythological place of the first dynasty of the Inca. Inca record keepers recount that at dawn on the solstice, the Earth opened up at the window of Pacaritanpu, and the first Inca, Manco Capac, stepped into this world and was engendered by a special ray of light. Then the brothers and sisters emerged and were also engendered by the sun, becoming the "illuminated ones," the Inca.

The constellation known as the Catachillay, or the llama, now known as the Coalsack and found in the southern part of the Milky Way below the Southern Cross, was also very important to the Inca, who associate the llama with water. According to their mythology, in the middle of a specific night in October the llama lowers its head to drink from the sea, an action that prevents the flooding of the world. To pay homage to this animal's function, on the side of one of the mountains at Ollantaytambo the Inca built a huge ceremonial space in the shape of a llama. The design is incredibly complex and has a powerful energy field that was intended for ritualistic use. Various parts of the llama correspond to elements of ritualistic structure: the eyes of the llama include an unfinished astronomical observatory; the head is the Temple of the Sun; the backbone is an ingenious walkway; and the genitals housed two granaries for the storage of seeds, one for the masculine and one for the feminine. In the days of the

Inca, the first light of day lit the latter granary, cosmically fertilizing the seed. Then the sunlight lit the eyes of the llama, wakening its consciousness. The association between the llama and water is also represented in the design since, in addition to other uses, the complex functioned as an observatory for determining the exact dates to hold ceremonies dedicated to requests for rain during the growing season.

The concept of "as above, so below" (the reflection of the sacred relationships here on Earth) permeated Andean culture, and the Inca thought of the combination of the Sacred Valley and the Vilcanota River as *huauque*, or double, of the Milky Way. Also central to the Andean worldview was the Incan term *yanantin*, or complementary pair. It is used to describe complements like masculine and feminine, and upper and lower—concepts our modern culture might consider opposites. However, the Inca strove to respect the apparent differences between complements and viewed them as part of a reflective whole.

Both of these concepts are apparent in the design of Machu Picchu. The landscape around Machu Picchu, as well as the monument itself, indicate a knowledge of sacred geometry. The two mountains at the site, Machu Picchu and Wayna Picchu, represent the divine complements, masculine and feminine, respectively. Lush and green, the whole site at Machu Picchu rises up from the rain forest as if reaching to the heavens. Through the site's physical beauty alone, it is possible to experience euphoria or be transported into a spiritual realm.

The Inca accentuated the mystical qualities already present in the landscape through their design of the sanctuary and ceremonial complex, which is shaped like a flying cayman, a very ancient symbol suggesting matter transformed to spirit and evoking a feeling of the transcendent Quetzalcoatl of Mesoamerica. In addition, the larger sanctuary is designed in the shape of a condor, a mystical bird flying to the spiritual world of the Milky Way, an amazing form that is superimposed on the image of the flying cayman. The gentle superimposition of man-made forms on natural forms expresses an extraordinary harmony between man and the divine. This sacred correspondence is one of the most precious legacies of humanity, one of tremendous spiritual significance.

There is a story associated with the majestic image of the condor (the divine messenger who embodies the sacred in the Incan worldview) flying toward the Milky Way. According to legend, whenever the seed of light falls into darkness, the great sun sends its messenger to the people in the form of a brilliant iridescent bird whose very presence brings a mysterious influence. Subsequently, violence, hatred, and anger are dissolved, and an atmosphere of love fills the air.[30]

Closing the Gateway to the Gods

The history of the Andes reveals that after Wiraccocha left the world about 650 A.D., large-scale, organized warfare, previously unknown in the Andes, became commonplace. Shortly thereafter the high civilization of Tiahuanaco collapsed, resulting in a profound transformation of the worldview of the Andean people.

According to archaeological records, warfare began in the central Andean region inhabited by the Wari[31]—a people who had a cosmology radically different from the advanced ancient civilizations they brutally conquered (including the Tiahuanaco). The Wari were a secular rather than a spiritual society. They conquered and ruled with violence and were obsessed with elitism, wealth, power, and control.[32] It is this image of ruthless warfare and sacrificial practice that our modern culture often falsely associates with the Inca.

By contrast, from the beginning of time (as measured by the coming of Wiraccocha) the indigenous people of the Andean highlands had lived in a manner taught by their god, based on classless cooperation between many ethnic groups and the principle of reciprocity. Their creator god, Wiraccocha, was seen as an androgynous being, and thus men and women were treated with equal respect; neither was dominant, and both sexes were seen as natural complements.

Tiahuanaco's influence, which extended throughout the surrounding region of present-day eastern and western Bolivia, northwestern Argentina, northern Chile, and southern Peru, had also not been achieved by warfare. The Tiahuanaco had no army, and their conquests were based on prestige and the fact that they shared their knowledge. Cooperative alliances were formed with regional communities that focused on loyalty, sharing resources, and the common good.[33]

Tiahuanaco's civic center, Akapana, was considered its greatest architectural achievement. It was a stepped, flat-topped pyramid from which water cascaded—a replica of the sacred cliff found on the Island of the Sun in Lake Titicaca, which is said to be the source of divine life.

According to archaeological findings, this golden age came to an abrupt end between A.D. 600 and A.D. 650 when every Tiahuanaco structure was destroyed by the Wari. Akapana and its elaborate water drainage system was closed and subsequently buried along with mutilated bodies and thousands of fragments of vessels bearing the Wari motif, painted bands of stylized human trophy heads.[34] The Wari reign of terror continued for some 200 years and completely transformed the high Andes. The floodwaters of carnage and destruction washed away all but the remnants of the Andean golden age.

When the Wari state finally collapsed in about A.D. 850, it left a legacy of many warring hamlets, each a hilltop fortress. Gone was the ceremonial and spiritual architecture of the golden age. The warrior classes that remained in control were all male-dominated jaguar cults who practiced animal sacrifices, as had the Wari. The light that Wiraccocha had brought to the world had grown dim. As ethnoastronomer William Sullivan points out, up until then the cosmology of the highland tribes had been based upon acting responsibly in all the three realms of Andean reality.[35] An evolved spiritual order had shaped society and brought balance to the people's lives. After spiritual order collapsed, this balanced perspective was almost entirely lost.

The people that we know as the Inca arose from the chaos that was the legacy of the Wari. According to Incan mythology, before Wiraccocha departed this world he gave his staff to a warrior chief named Apotambo. This staff represented the lineage of light. In time, the first Inca were born of this lineage. Historically, the first Inca, Manco Capac, who was known as the mythical founder of the dynasty, appeared about A.D. 1200.

It is apparent that the Inca built on the accomplishments of the earlier culture of Tiahuanaco. Although Incan myths, their theology, and to a large extent their social structure were derived from their predecessors, neither their artwork nor their monuments matched the splendor of the golden age. The Incan royalty considered themselves to be of divine descent and were perceived as gods by their subjects. Only the royalty were known as "Inca." This belief in their natural superiority paved the way for the creation of an empire. Although the empire was not built without bloodshed, many tribes simply acquiesced to what they perceived as the Incan superiority.

The *wakas*, customs, and languages of most conquered tribes were maintained as part of a higher order. The Inca had an elaborate education system, primarily for the royalty and the administrative class. High arts were well developed, and the Virgins of the Sun, the *mamacona,* were particularly known for their fine textiles and other arts.

The wealth of the Empire of the Sun was measured not so much by the monuments the Inca built but by the well-being they generated. They chose to expand their empire by building elaborate terraces and complex systems of irrigation, perhaps their greatest monuments. They used land to create surpluses for their 6 million people and to avoid famines.[36]

In a few decades they established an empire the size of the Roman Empire, extending about 2,500 miles from present-day Columbia to southern Chile. They built over 10,000 miles of roads and had a communication system that allowed foot messengers to travel through the jungles and the high mountains, running up to 150 miles per day. Astonishingly, they did this all without iron, horses, wheels, or a written language.

Like their predecessors, the Inca lacked a written language, and records were kept by the *quipus,* knotted cords. The people who understood the meaning of the knots were their historians. Later, during the Spanish conquest, the Spanish burned most of the *quipus* and killed many record keepers, severely limiting our knowledge of Incan civilization.[37]

Pachacuti—A Time of Transformation

All existing written records of Incan life were composed by clergy and others after the Spanish conquest, and, with few exceptions, none of these sources tells about the Incan civilization without extreme cultural bias. In an effort to obtain a less biased perspective on the Incan worldview, ethnoastronomer William Sullivan has focused on Incan mythology. In *The Secret of the Incas,* he successfully chronicles Andean history through a synthesis of Incan myths and archaeoastronomy.

As is true of the Maya of the classical period, Sullivan found that the story of the Inca was told in the stars. But instead of analyzing creation myths, he focused on stories that recorded the times of *pachacuti,* the times when the Incan world underwent great transformation. To the Inca, a *pachacuti* was a time when their perception of reality was overturned, marking the advent of a new world-age, or a new sun. Sullivan found that these periods were accurately reflected in many of their myths.

The first of these periods is known as the *ukhupachacuti*, a transformation of reality by means of water.[38] This flood is referenced in many Incan stories. Perhaps the most common myth tells of a llama who gradually became more and more despondent and would not eat. When the shepherd at last asked the llama what was wrong, the llama replied that the conjunction of the stars foretold that the world would soon be destroyed by a flood. Sullivan found that this flood occurred in A.D. 650. When he studied the sky for the June solstice of 650 A.D., he discovered that the stars did indeed reveal a time of *pachacuti*. He saw that in the southern Andes for the first time in more than 800 years, the Milky Way ceased to rise heliacally at the June solstice. Thus, there was a cosmic marker for the end of the third or golden age when Tiahuanaco was destroyed. As shown by the historical record, this marker also coincided with the rise of the Wari state and the appearance of aggressive warrior cults that brought the fourth sun. The myths tell that this was also the time Wiraccocha left the world and went back to the place of his origin, crossing the bridge in the Milky Way that led to the land of the gods.

There were two primary threads that held the Inca to their worldview. One was a gateway to the gods (Wiraccocha) that allowed direct contact between the divine and human beings. The second thread was another gateway of sorts that allowed the Inca access to their ancestors, the seat of all their culture and teachings. In time, both of these threads would be lost, and the Inca would say that the gateways had indeed closed.

Because we live in the Milky Way, we do not see its entirety—only its branches. The two seasonal branches visible in the night sky were called gateways (of the first sort mentioned above) by the Inca. Sullivan has found that the sky map indicates precisely that this gateway closed on A.D. June 20, 650, for on that date, for the first time in history, the predecessors of the Inca could no longer see the Milky Way on the morning of the winter solstice. This precessional event was later recorded in myth. With the closing of this gateway, the sacred worldview of the Tiahuanaco was displaced by that of the barbaric Wari. The threads that connected the Tiahuanaco to their deeper knowledge began to unravel.

However, the gateway to the ancestors (the second type of gateway mentioned above) remained open. The Inca worshiped their ancestors and turned to them for wisdom and guidance. It was the ancestors who had maintained the fragile thread of their divine lineage, connecting them to their mystical traditions. But this thread that had survived the ravages of *pachacuti* was now threatened. What remained of their sacred traditions was about to be lost in another great flood.

Wiraccocha Inca, the eighth Incan ruler was known as a great oracle and allegedly had the power to hurl great balls of fire at his enemies.[39] It was during his reign that the ominous signs of the end of the Incan world were first foretold in the night sky. During this time period, it was apparent that the Milky Way would soon no longer be visible on either solstice. This precessional event was later coded in Andean myth. The legends also foretold that the great celestial llama, which, each night in October, drank the water of the celestial river so that this space/time would not be flooded, was endangered. The Inca saw this precessional event as a sign of the prophecy of the end of their culture.

This was the atmosphere in which the ninth Inca, known as Pachacuti Inca, seized the reins of power and forged the Empire of the Children of the Sun, the largest empire that the world had ever known. It is said that both Pachacuti Inca and his father Wiraccocha Inca had the powers of god-men and that Pachacuti Inca was assisted in his victories by the gods. Pachacuti Inca was called the great earth-shaker because he attempted to overturn space/time. He refused to accept the fatalism of his father's era that arose from the night sky's prophecy. Instead he declared a new world-age, the fifth sun. To effect this great change, he demoted the priests of the warrior clans and revived the teachings of Wiraccocha, who had remained the god of the peasantry but not the upper classes.

Pachacuti Inca was incredibly gutsy. According to legend, on an ominous day he went to the Sapi stone, high above Cuzco, where he met with the great Wiraccocha himself and bargained with the creator god until an agreement was reached to delay the end of Incan civilization three more generations. Then Pachacuti Inca, his son Tupa Inca, and his grandson Huayna Capac Inca proceeded to build a great empire. It was not until the death of his grandson that the entire empire was once again facing ruin.

Pachacuti Inca acted fearlessly and desperately in his attempt to forestall destruction of the Incan worldview. While he may have been a compassion-ate ruler who spiritually revitalized the Inca and built Machu Picchu, he also instituted inhumane and barbaric practices. He ordered a reorganization of all the *wakas*, the statues that connected the people to their divine origins in the stars. He then created the rite of *capacocha*, human sacrifice. Previously, there had been no significant history of sacrifice among the Inca. The *capacocha* was held at the December solstice. For this rite, caravans of gold, silver, and textiles were sent to Cuzco from each lineage and offered to the gods. Most importantly, fair and unblemished children from each royal lineage,[40] the finest god-seeds of the Empire of the Children of the Sun, were sacrificed at the sacred places in the name of their lineage *wakas*.[41] They were, as Sullivan states, sent as emissaries to each of the stars connected to their lineage *waka* bearing desperate messages.[42] They were sent home to plead for their culture's survival.

By between 1525 and 1527, Pachacuti Inca's heir—Huayna Capac Inca—lay dying of smallpox in Quito.[43] It is said that Huayna Capac Inca died 17 years later with the prophecy of his great-grandfather on his lips, knowing he would be the last Inca before the next flood. He told his sons to serve the invaders whom he envisioned as new Wiraccochas. The Inca held the belief that Wiraccocha would one day return. Similarly, the Indians of Mesoamerica believed in the prophesied return of Quetzalcoatl from across the great water. These long-standing beliefs explain why Cortez was hailed as a returning god. Belief in the return of the great white brothers, the mythical god-men, hastened the downfall of both the Aztec and the Inca.[44]

Uneasiness and despair continued to engulf the empire. There were unsettling reports of supernatural occurrences, earthquakes, comets, and rings around the moon. The moment that the king of birds, an eagle who had been pursued by several hawks, fell lifeless in the great Cuzco square in the midst of Incan nobility, it could no longer be denied. The end of the empire was approaching.[45]

On the December solstice of 1432, the gateway to the ancestors closed—the date Wiraccocha Inca had foreseen as the end of time. When Sullivan studied the December solstice sky of Cuzco for 1432, he found that the portion of the Milky Way along the ecliptic at the horizon was barely visible. Just to the south was the celestial llama, and the floodwaters of time were indeed rising.[46]

The Seed Awaits Reawakening

The myths left as a legacy by the Inca were mnemonic devices used to record the history of the people of the high Andes in a way that would survive the destruction of their culture that came with a new sun. Their sky maps, celestial references found in myth marking the progression of the stars, were another form of mnemonic coding. As discussed, the Inca believed that the natural world had patterns that corresponded to those of a higher order of intelligence,[47] and they built their ceremonial centers to reflect such sacred correspondences. Being seeds of the divine, they looked to the heavens for guidance and for indications of the intent of the creator.

As Sullivan points out, there was a curious but undeniable correlation between astronomical events and the unfolding of Incan history. The transformations that occurred in the Incan world seemed to correlate with how the solstice suns entered and left the Milky Way. This synchronicity began in the year 200 B.C. when the solstice sun first entered the Milky Way. According to Incan myths, it was at this time that the bridge to the land of the gods opened, and Wiraccocha entered this world. Then, after civilization developed, Tiahuanaco arose and experienced a golden age, which ended in about A.D. 650 with the advent of warfare with the Wari people. In the sky at that time, the June solstice sun no longer entered the Milky Way; the gateway to the gods was closed. Finally in 1544, with the death of Huayna Capac Inca, and with the Milky Way no longer at all visible at the June solstice, time ended. The Spanish arrived and devastated the empire.

The rational, Western interpretation of the fall of the Incan empire would no doubt be that it was due to extreme cultural delusion and fatalism. However, this view is too simplistic and myopic. The Incan culture was shamanic, with shamanic perception that had been developed through extensive training. Perhaps, as Sullivan suggests, the Inca were not fatalistic but had advanced abilities that enabled them to perceive the unfolding higher order within chaos.[48] Whatever the facts, it is clear that the close of their cycle of time was marked by catastrophic world and cosmic events that foretold the end of their culture.

After Huayna Capac Inca's death, there was a great civil war instigated by two of his sons who were would-be successors. In addition, smallpox had ravaged the entire empire, and the Inca were resigned to their fate as a result of their cosmological understanding. Consequently, conquest by the Spanish was swift and as brutal as the Wari campaigns. With a mere 175 men, Francisco Pizarro devastated an empire of over 6 million people.

During the conquest, the Spanish, directed by the Catholic Church, systematically destroyed nearly all vestiges of Incan spiritual life: every lineage *waka*, every *intihuatana* stone, all the ceremonial sites, and the *quipus*. Moreover, the conquistadors invaded sanctuaries of the Virgins of the Sun, whom they raped. The agricultural terraces and irrigation systems were seized but were not maintained. As a result, the people were no longer connected to the stars from which they originated; the solstices and equinoxes so vital to the people's vision could no longer be accurately observed; the people's ties with history were severed; and there were no longer any surpluses of food or water but instead droughts and famines. The conquistadors, driven by overwhelming greed and a blind arrogance based on an indoctrinated sense of moral superiority, had but two interests: subjugation and gold.

The story in Mesoamerica is much the same as that in Peru, although in both regions, even long after their golden ages, the civilizations overrun by the Spanish were in many ways far more advanced and progressive than the cities of Spain at that time.[49] Since the Vatican had decreed that the indigenous people of the Americas were not human and thus had no souls, anything was tolerated in the blind pursuit of the one and only god—gold. From Cuzco alone, the Spanish took billions of dollars worth of gold, often in the form of extraordinary pieces of artwork melted into ingots.[50] Much of the wealth that came from the conquests ended up in the coffers of the Catholic Church, which, in turn, continued to support the conquistadors.

Ultimately, the goal of the conquistadors was to break the spirit of the people. They were enslaved and brutalized, stripped of everything that had meaning, and their religious practices were outlawed. However, despite this violence, the seed did not die, but instead went underground, within the unconscious, where in the realm of our deepest yearnings it awaited the return of the light.

4

ANDEAN
PROPHECIES OF
A NEW AGE

IN 1949 AN ANTHROPOLOGIST FROM CUZCO NAMED
Dr. Oscar Nuñez del Prado attended a festival in Paucartambo, located in
the eastern Andes in southern Peru due east of Cuzco. There he overheard
two regal-looking Indians speaking in what he recognized as a pure
Quechua dialect, the language of the Inca. Anthropologists had believed
this pure dialect was no longer in use, and he was excited about the probability that these Indians might have preserved other cultural vestiges of
the ancient Inca.[1]

In 1955, Oscar Nuñez del Prado led the first known Western expedi-
tion to the modern home of the Q'ero people, some 600 of which were
found living at altitudes above 14,000 feet in five small villages, in a manner very similar to that of their ancestors (possibly the Inca).

Today, the Q'ero continue to tend their flocks as they have always done,
migrating seasonally from elevations of 5,000 feet to elevations of over
14,000 feet. At lower elevations at the edge of the jungle, they plant corn and
other food crops, while at higher elevations they graze their herds. They
spin and weave the wool used in their clothing, which is made in traditional Incan styles. The Q'ero are simple farmers and expert weavers. They

have endured great hardships and brutal suppression, yet they have managed to retain key aspects of the ancient ways, preserving the essence of the Andean mystical path. Since they have lived for some twenty generations in isolated high mountain villages, more of their traditions and worldview survived the Spanish conquest, the Inquisition, and the indoctrination by the Catholic Church than did the traditions of other Andeans, whose worldviews were eroded due to cultural interaction and assimilation.

There are many who believe the Q'ero may be the direct descendants of the Inca.[2] As it turns out, the Inca, the remnant sacred seed of an ancient seeded culture, were enslaved by their conquerors but perhaps never vanquished. Instead, they went underground and into isolation. As stated in Wayu's story in Chapter 1, the seed was buried deep within the earth, where it lay dormant through the long night until awakened by the light of a new sun.

Andean Teachings

Many people have helped bring the teachings of the Q'ero and the elements of Andean mysticism to the world. Among them is anthropologist, author, and teacher Alberto Villoldo, who founded the Four Winds Society, dedicated to preserving Q'ero teachings, and who studied with several Q'ero masters. Americo Yabar, a mestizo and one of several Q'ero-trained practitioners, travels worldwide disseminating Q'ero teachings. Author Joan Parisi Wilcox, herself a fourth-level Andean priest, has interviewed many Q'ero mystics and presented their teachings in a manner accessible to the general population. In addition, Elizabeth Jenkins, author and director of the Wiroquocha Foundation, which works to preserve indigenous wisdom, writes and teaches workshops about Q'ero beliefs. Wilcox's and Jenkins' primary teacher, Juan Nuñez del Prado, is the son of Oscar Nuñez del Prado, the anthropologist who discovered the Q'ero. Juan is also an Andean priest who was trained by the Q'ero and a parallel Incan priesthood that survived the Spanish conquest. Through workshops and accounts of personal experiences with the Q'ero in worlds beyond time as we know it, these people have made the perspective of the Q'ero fathomable and alive.

In recent years the diverse cultures of the Andes have begun to reclaim their ancient mystical heritage. Andean priests once again conduct rituals of ancient origin at sacred Incan sites. The teachings surrounding these rituals were kept alive by the isolated Q'ero and other practitioners. They were practiced quietly and transmitted orally within the priesthood. Aspects of ancient rituals and beliefs were also hidden behind the mask of Catholicism, as anyone who visits the Catholic churches of Peru and Mesoamerica can quickly perceive.

What we can learn from Andean mysticism is amazing. However, to grasp even the basics of their teachings we need to step outside the little box of limited perception that makes up what we call reality and learn to perceive our world—as they do—in terms of living energy fields. This involves learning to see the energy that exists behind all forms in the manner that Juan Nuñez del Prado instructs his students, not with our physical eyes but with our spiritual or third eye. This avenue of perception is what the Andean people call *gawag*, an ability that leads to direct perception and interaction with the world of living energies.[3]

Today, we can better understand the worldview of the Inca and other ancient people of the Peruvian highlands. The Q'ero perspective and the Andean mystical heritage confirms that the Inca saw the world in a radically different way than we do—in multiple realities. According to Yabar, the *panya* is the ordinary world.[4] We can think of the ordinary world as the reality that exists in linear time, the reality we perceive with the five senses. The *yoge* is the world of nonordinary perception that exists on many levels outside of linear time, and it can be perceived energetically through direct experience. A more precise view however involves the understanding that these concepts refer to the complementary pathways of learning found in Andean mysticism. The *yoge* is the left side of the path and involves practical skills like healing but also the more wild aspects of the path. The *panya* is the right-sided path, connected with the left brain. Related to mystical teachings, ceremony, and ritual, it is more ordered and structured.[5] To the Andeans and the Q'ero, everything consists of energy and is animate—even manufactured items like houses, weavings, tools, and machines. In this context, it is interesting to note that scientists working at the frontiers of knowledge are suggesting that consciousness may be an aspect of all matter.

From the Andean perspective, the energetic aspect of an object or entity can not only be perceived but also interacted with. *Kausay pacha* is the Quechua expression for the energy universe. The living energy of the *kausay pacha* is neither positive nor negative, but variations can be distinguished by their density, weight, or refinement, and there can be many subtle distinctions within a given field of energy.

Furthermore, the *kausay pacha* exists within a three-tiered cosmology. Each plane of existence has specific energetic characteristics. The first plane is called the *ukhupacha* (*pacha* means cosmos or earth in Quechua) and is known as the interior world, or the underworld. This plane exists both within the Earth, the individual psyche, and the cosmos. While it is not a parallel concept to the Christian hell, the heaviest, least refined energies are found in the *ukhupacha*. These energies may be considered thought forms or invisible spirits.

The second plane is called the *kaypacha* and is the realm of our everyday material reality. The plants, water, sky, earth, and animals that sustain us are all part of the *kaypacha*. It contains the totality of the *pachamama*, the great Cosmic Mother, including Mother Earth, who is considered the source of all life and the feminine aspect of cosmic energy. Both refined and heavy energies are found on the second plane. It is interesting to compare the concept of *pachamama* with the popular Gaia hypothesis, which suggests that the entire earth may be a living organism. This idea developed from James Lovelock's observation that our planet is a self-regulating system based on his evaluation of its carbon, nitrogen, and oxygen systems and cycles. It is supported by the work of many others in related fields, including Lynn Margulis and Lewis Thomas. By contrast, the *pachamama* is a broader concept which includes all physical manifestation in the universe.

The third plane of the Andean world is called the *hanaqpacha* or superior world and is the realm of the most refined energies. The superior world is inhabited only by highly refined spiritual beings that may be perceived as deities, angels, the high Inca, the saints of the Christian world, or sacred images. The energy of this world can be experienced personally or collectively. The miraculous apparitions of Mary at Fatima, Lourdes, Medjugorje, and elsewhere are examples of a collective experience of the superior world.

The mystical, nonordinary realities of the *yoge* and *panya* (not associated with any one particular plane) occur outside of linear time and can be accessed through higher aspects of the self. While many of the old teachings have not survived, some among the Q'ero, like the Inca before them, are capable of accessing multiple selves. While one self functions within the flow of linear time, other selves function in the simultaneous realities of dreamtime, sacred time, or ritual time.[6]

"Shaman" and "shamanic" have become overused catchall terms which imply that higher realities can only be accessed by highly trained, elite individuals. However, it is important to note that the types of perceptions associated with the *yoge* and the *panya* are not limited to highly trained shamans and mystics. Indeed, in many ancient cultures the shamanic state was a widespread cultural worldview.

In fact, the superior world is accessible to everyone. All individuals can learn to discriminate between refined and heavy energies and perceive energy in individuals as well as in places and objects. For example, most people can readily perceive heavy energy when they are around someone who is angry or troubled, and refined energy when they walk into a temple or a meditation room.

In an article about the Q'ero worldview written for *Magical Blend*, expressing the view of Alberto Villoldo, Joan Parisi Wilcox wrote:

> ...the Q'ero belief system is one that is largely undiluted and uncontaminated by logic, reason, or violence... They have not lost the sensory foundation of knowledge nor replaced their mythological perceptual stance with the cognitive view as the West has done.

> ...Culturally and certainly shamanically, they tend not to make the Cartesian distinction between subject and object, between inner and outer, between the signified and the signifier, between the secular and the sacred. Thus they are able to slip the bounds of the causal and are able to literally step outside of linear, monochronic time into nonlinear polychronic time. They have not lost the sensory foundation of knowledge, and so they perceive synthesthetically—bridging the five senses, so that looking at a mountain they can feel its texture. They perceive totalities, which are by definition, nonlinear, rather than the fragmented, causal realities the West apprehends.[7]

Andean masters have learned to navigate the worlds of the *yoge* and the *panya* with ease. After a while such multi-dimensional functioning can become second nature—it is only a matter of perception. The difference between most people and those with shamanic abilities lies in the development of perception. Shamans can discriminate between states that we can barely conceive of, due in part to their strong focus and clear intentions that allow them to shape their reality. By contrast, most of us are shaped by ours.

To navigate in nonordinary realities, we need to alter the concepts we have about ourselves and others. The conceptual framework we have been taught by our parents and our culture is based upon perception of ordinary reality. Not only are we taught to perceive primarily through our five senses, we are also taught to rely almost exclusively on our sense of sight. If we can't see it, we believe it does not exist. We are also stuck perceptually within the confines of linear time. But what if we could see the world energetically and multi-dimensionally? What if we too could "step beyond linear time"? To some extent, many of us have already had experiences that give us a glimpse of dimensions beyond ordinary perception—experiences our rational mind has denied or minimized. Such experiences sometimes occur during meditation, through the discovery of gateways to a higher world; or through inspired writing, music, or artwork. On such occasions we experience the essential truth of existence, what the Q'ero and the Inca before them called the *kausay pacha,* the energy universe.

Fortunately, the potential for such a broader perception is not limited to the stalwart few who, as did Carlos Castaneda, pass the rigors of the shamanic path. Instead, such an expanded sense of reality is widely accessible if we can break free of our own self-limiting concepts.

Q'ero-trained Americo Yabar states that those of us who have been indoctrinated by the Western system of thought must begin by reconnecting with the *pachamama,* the Cosmic Mother. Western thought is built on a very limited perceptual foundation that may have been revolutionary in the 1600s when René Descartes envisioned a mechanistic, predictable universe based on Cartesian coordinates. But we have outgrown this simplistic reasoning. We now understand, at least theoretically, that mind and matter are implicitly connected. But the damage caused by the mechanical model has been done. Our task now is to heal the wounds in our psyche caused by the Cartesian split, a split that literally tore us from the breast of the divine Cosmic Mother.

In an interview with Hal Zina Bennett for *Shaman's Drum*, Yabar describes the situation as follows:

> *The message of the Q'ero is that people need to reconnect with the matrix of the cosmos—with the spirit of* Pachamama *which is the Earth; with the spirits of the mountains, or* apus, *and the spirit of the stars.*
>
> *We know that the Andes is a source of tremendous spiritual light and that these filaments of light—or threads of energy— are part of a tapestry of spiritual awakening across the planet, the birthing of a new light on Earth....*
>
> *There is already a network of very strong spiritual energy happening on the planet now. But we need to meditate, to reflect on it. There are many kinds of meditation, but the form I am speaking of involves meditating on being in the lap of the* Pachamama, *the Mother Earth, the Cosmic Mother. This form starts with meditating on the simple but profound awareness that we are living on the lap of the* Pachamama *and we feed ourselves from her strength.*
>
> *Once you feel the* Pachamama *you begin to have a very clear awareness of your place on the planet. This is why we work with the* Pachamama, *the Cosmic Mother, the mother of all mothers.*"[8]

Thus the concept of *pachamama* is crucial for achieving a perspective of a multi-dimensional reality.

Another idea useful for gaining such a perspective is *ayni,* which means reciprocity or exchange of energy. This principle is derived from the Andean perception of "energy beyond form" and is practiced between individuals and with all of nature. The goal of the practice is to walk in perfect harmony (*ayni*) in all three levels of existence.

The practice of *ayni* involves communicating and sending your love to another, whether it is the earth, another person, a dog, or a tree. Although this is done without expectation in the pure spirit of giving, each time you practice *ayni,* miraculously you do receive something back.

Ayni is described by one of Villoldo's Q'ero teachers, Antonio Morales as follows:

> *... The Sun is the father and the Earth is the mother and their*
> *parents are one—Illa Tici Viracocha [Wiraccocha]—neither male*
> *nor female, energy in its purest form.... This is the basis of all*
> *Andean shamanism. It is a principle of reciprocity. You make*
> *ayni to the Pachamama, the Mother Earth, and she is pleased*
> *and returns your gift with fertility and abundance. You make ayni*
> *to the Sun, and he returns your gift with warmth and light.*
> *The Apus, the great mountain peaks, give you strength to*
> *endure your work; the heavens give you harmony. Make ayni*
> *to all people and they will honor you in return. It is a wonderful*
> *principle.*
>
> *They say that the shaman lives in perfect ayni—the universe*
> *reciprocates his every action, mirrors his intent back to him, as*
> *he is a mirror to others. That is why the shaman lives in*
> *synchronicity with Nature. The shaman's world mirrors*
> *the shaman's will and intent and actions.*[9]

Morales states that perfect *ayni* comes directly from the heart. It is not necessary to analyze our response. Only then is the world a true reflection of our love and our action. This grand and ancient principle was even immortalized in the late 1960s by the Beatles and the love generation. Even if only for a brief moment it seems we understood "that the love you take is equal to the love you make."[10] The Andeans see themselves as living in an energetic universe, where the goal of all activity is harmonious interchange of energy between the self and all others and all of nature. In time the practice of *ayni* can become automatic, a way of living and perceiving. As Morales states:

> *... Eventually we make ayni because we must, because we feel it*
> *in here [in our hearts]. They say that only then is ayni perfect,*
> *but I believe that ayni is always perfect, that our world is always*
> *a true reflection of our intent and our love and our actions.*
> *That is my opinion, but I think that it is a good one. The*
> *condition of our world depends upon the condition of our*
> *consciousness, of our souls."*[11]

When we walk in perfect *ayni*, everything is sacred. We perceive, think, act, and speak from the heightened understanding of the sacred nature of all of existence. The world then mirrors back to us what we are—also sacred.

Another related concept central to understanding the Andean world-view is that relationships can be perceived in terms of energy. From this per-spective there are three stages of every relationship, each of which can be perceived energetically. This is true whether the relationship is between predator and prey, teacher and student, two peers, two nations, or two lovers.

The first stage is the encounter called *tinkuy*. The two energy fields make contact, that is, they actually touch. If the energy fields choose to interact, they interweave, connecting energetically. This interweaving may cause a feeling of uneasiness, particularly in a new relationship.

The second stage interaction, which in the West is often a confronta-tion, is called *tupay*. This interaction between two entities unknown to each other is not necessarily unfriendly or aggressive but can be more like sizing up the other and the potential for interaction. In Andean thought this concept is commonly illustrated by the story of two Indians who meet on a trail and check each other out, eyeing each other, smelling each other, and challenging each other through body language.[12] These actions are not perceived as aggressive behavior on the part of either individual. In the Andean tradition, power is displayed in the manner of friendly com-petition, as a way to learn about the other. This learning may take the form of competition in which there will be a winner, such as a race to the top of the mountain.

The difference between the Andean concept of relationship and ours is that theirs does not focus on one-upmanship. Once there is a winner in competition, the third stage of a relationship, communion, or *taqe,* occurs. In this stage, any winner of a competition is obligated to teach the other. During *taqe*, the filaments of the two separate energy bodies actually blend together and a type of energetic communion takes place. As a result, the luminous bodies of the two individuals gain mutual understanding and reach a new level of cooperation.

Incan leaders demonstrated the practice of *taqe* in their treatment of the cultures they conquered, which became part of their empire. Other cul-tures were allowed to maintain their beliefs and thus their cultural identity. There were almost a hundred separate ethnic groups in the empire, each of which spoke dozens of dialects. Their individual customs were treated respectfully; they were given food, land, and taught the traditional arts.

According to Incan beliefs, those who have achieved a broader perception or have a higher consciousness practice *taqe*, the joining of energy fields for the purpose of uplifting humanity. It is in the spirit of *taqe* that the Andean practitioners are sharing their prophecies, for they understand that this is the time of the Taqe Onkay, the great interweaving of the tribes.

Andean Prophecies

The Andean prophecies are centered on the concept of transformation, or *pachacuti*. *Pacha* means cosmos or Earth, while *cuti* means to turn upside down or to set right. Pachacuti was the name given to the ninth Inca ruler, who built Machu Picchu and the Empire of the Children of the Sun. As the name implies he was a transformer of Incan society who initiated the Incan fifth world age, or the fifth sun, which ironically also brought the end of the Incan world. The time of the *pachacuti* brought the arrival of the Spanish conquistadors and ultimately the destruction of the empire. In a fury of violence, the highest cultural order the Andes had ever known was swiftly overturned.

The Andean prophecies predict the return of *pachacuti*, but these are not prophecies of doom—they promise a new human beginning, "a millennium of gold in the Earth."[13] They speak of the potential that comes from "stepping outside of time,"[14] which is not merely a metaphoric concept but a concrete achievement that can awaken all the people of the world.

When we step outside of time, we let go of all past concepts and all perception resulting from our usual notion of time and space. Such a shift gives us the potential to recreate ourselves in an entirely new paradigm. The prophecies according to Villoldo speak of a "tear in the fabric of time."[15] The Andean elders recognize that this event, which is a perceptual phenomenon, presents humanity with an enormous opportunity. If we are able to let go of every limiting concept that we have about ourselves, we will finally see the full splendor of what we can be—what people of the Incan culture have always known. We are, in effect, divine seeds of light—we are god-seeds.

The Andean prophecies imply that the gateways to other dimensions are opening again. Americo Yabar refers to the current time of *pachacuti* as "the

time of the new seed." The resulting new humanity will be capable of perceiving the universe in a radically different way; we will be able to step outside of linear time. When we slip through the gateways to other dimensions,
we have the opportunity, as did Wayu, to explore our full human potential.

The prophecies also speak of the time of the *mastay,* or the reintegration of the peoples of the four directions. The Q'ero and other Andeans
have offered their teachings to help the world prepare for the great *mastay.* As they express it, the time is coming for the Great Eagle of the North
and the Great Condor of the South (referring to the Americas as a whole)
to fly together again.[16]

The Andean teachings involve *mosoq karpay,* a special ceremony in
which the seed of *pachacuti* is said to be placed in the luminous body of
each recipient, thus through an energetic transmission, connecting the
individual with the power of the ancient lineage, the seedbed of Wiraccocha. Within the seed are the light codes of the body of the Inca, the god-
being connected directly to the stars.

There are many paths to awakening the seed of divinity in all of us.
Through prayer (sacred speech), through ceremony and ritual (sacred
actions), by means of direct transmission (sacred grace), and by practic-
ing *ayni* (sacred being), the seeds within us can awaken and prosper. However, these seeds will not awaken until we shed the false beliefs that tell us
we stand apart from nature. To awaken, we need to break out of the limited Cartesian worldview and reunite with the divine Cosmic Mother.
Ironically, only through Eve can we regain our entry into the garden.

In this context, Alberto Villoldo claims that to gain such expanded
awareness westerners first need to shed the myth that we were kicked out
of the garden. He says: "We are the only people in the world who were cast
out. All primitive people have an immediate communion in the garden:
They still walk in the garden, they still talk to the trees, the rivers, and the
rivers talk back to them."[17]

Once we are able to dismiss the myth of our banishment, there is no
need for self-negating theologies or psychologies. We are then whole—how
we started out and how we are now. As Americo Yabar tells us, to nurture the
seed we must first reconnect with the *pachamama.* We need to offer to the
pachamama our highest *ayni.* This may be the single most important thing
we can do, both individually and as a human community.

The Andean holistic view of the importance of interrelationships also extends to types of people or cultures. In this view there are three types of people—those who have knowledge, known as the *yachay*; those who have love and feeling, known as the *munay;* and those who have the ability to manifest, known as the *llankay.* European people are said to most embody the great intellectual power of the *yachay.* The people of North America are said to have the most developed physical power and the strong will that leads to action in the external world, corresponding to the *llankay.* And the Indians of South America are said to possess the greatest love, representing the *munay.* However, according to the Andean viewpoint, no one ability is superior or complete in itself. People of all these qualities complement each other, and only when all three modalities work together will there be a unified humanity.

In addition, and most importantly, these three aspects—mind, body, and heart—like the three symbolic stones the Maya set on their hearths, must be blended within each individual. Imbalances within individuals, within separate cultures, and within humanity as a whole must be corrected.

The ancient Andean concept of relationship has a lot to offer our modern world. It stresses that we must all work together cooperatively and bring our individual and collective strengths and weaknesses together in the spirit of exchange and reciprocity. Only through the spirit of reciprocity will we as individuals and as humanity find completion.

The prophecies speak of events occurring within the collective. Although we must all work on an individual level to open our perceptual horizons and to find our own way of perfect *ayni,* it will be a collective humanity that will make the leap to a new level of consciousness. To achieve this, we need to use our collective intent to achieve perfect *ayni* with all nature, the *pachamama.*

The prophecies demonstrate the principles of *ayni,* reciprocity, and relationship. However, to comprehend the prophecies, it is necessary to understand the levels of development of consciousness along the Andean path, which are universal and can be achieved through many spiritual teachings.

According to the Andean perspective there are seven levels of consciousness. In her book *Initiation,* Elizabeth Jenkins describes her work with Juan Nuñez del Prado and the different levels of consciousness taught by him. According to Juan Nuñez del Prado, the majority of humanity has not moved beyond the third level of consciousness—a level mired in fear, conflict, violence, and spiritual impoverishment. Because the world mirrors back to us what we believe and embody, if humanity's actions and thoughts arise from fear, conflict, violence, and spiritual impoverishment, the universe will mirror such intent and actions. In this sense we create our own karma, and the future will always be a reflection of what we set in motion in the present. Consequently, until we are able to resolve fear, conflict, violence, and spiritual impoverishment within ourselves, we will be unable to move beyond the third level of consciousness.

To achieve the fourth level of consciousness, we must learn to let go of the heavy energies within us and heal the emotional wounds within our energy bodies, including the damage caused by our family and ancestral history. This is similar to the Toltec perspective which states that we need to rid ourselves of the limited beliefs we have absorbed from our culture and remove the residue of past reincarnations.

At first glance this might seem impossible, but it is not. It can be done by learning to work in harmony with the invisible universe, what the Andean path calls the energy universe. However, to work with the energy universe we must first restore our connection with the *pachamama*.

At the fourth level, we learn to work with the dynamics of our own energy body. Once we have learned to release our heavy energy we can work with the more refined energies of the *pachamama* and access the energies of the superior world. These energies can often be perceived in sacred areas where there are openings to the higher worlds. The fourth level also involves learning to perceive and work with the energy of individuals, groups, and sacred spaces. At the fourth level of consciousness we learn to surrender to the higher will. When we are able to do this, the energy itself guides us.

To achieve the fourth level of consciousness, we must work in *yanantin*, the state of harmonious relationship between different energies. A part of *yanantin* is learning to access, awaken, and respect both our inner masculine and feminine aspects as well as walk in perfect *ayni* with members of the opposite sex. We must learn to mirror with perfect *ayni* the love of the *pachamama*, the love of the other, and the love of the group. We can then begin to awaken the potential of the fifth level of consciousness.

Most Andean mystics do not believe there are individuals currently functioning at the fifth level of consciousness. However, some people believe that those among us who have gone beyond our individual karma have achieved the fifth level. This perspective implies that the great planetary healers and teachers of our modern time, such as H. H. the Dalai Lama and Sai Baba, are all functioning on the fifth level of consciousness and beyond. Their emergence in the human family marks a turning point for humanity. Although there have always been beings of great light on Earth in the past, they were legendary god-men. As more and more humans reach the fifth level of consciousness, we will enter into a new phase of human development. We may view this as a critical turn upon the spiral path of evolution. The light that through the process of involution entered deeply into matter will begin the process of ascension. Teachers at the fifth level of consciousness know how to work with the energy currents of their students' bodies, rebalancing and awakening energy filaments. They are also able to cleanse the residue of karma on an individual level and remove negative elements from humanity on a group level, thus making global transformation possible.

Juan Nuñez del Prado says that according to Andean prophecy individuals at the fifth level of consciousness will begin to emerge at the annual Festival of the Q'ollorit'i, or Festival of the Snow Star, high in the Andes, when the group energy generated by the festival is strong enough.[18] Specifically, the prophecy relates that the first male will arise at the Festival of the Q'ollorit'i and will walk to the town of Urcos by a given route. Then he will meet the second male by the door of a church near the temple of Wiraccocha. Together they will go to Cuzco to meet the third and then to Lima to meet the fourth. In Lima the four will meet the first female of the fifth level. Then they will go to Arequipa and encounter the second female. (The Inca culture was not patriarchal, having a creator god who was androgynous. While each Inca ruler had a female counterpart, they were not co-rulers but functioned in complementary domains like the sun and the moon that they allegedly represented.) From there, they will continue to Lake Titicaca, where they will meet the third female and then return to Cuzco, where they will encounter the fourth female, for a total of eight individuals. These eight will be joined by two more couples, from the North, for a total of twelve people at the fifth level of consciousness. Together the twelve will return to the Temple of Wiraccocha, where they will perform the ancient coronation ritual.

It is said that the last Inca, Huayna Capac Inca, the grandson of the great Pachacuti Inca, was selected during the coronation ritual at the temple of Wiraccocha, which has twelve temples, one for each royal Incan lineage. In the ceremony, twelve Inca, one from each of the royal lineages came together to select their next leader, the Sapa Inca. Reputedly, the candidate chosen was not only the best leader but also the most spiritually developed. The word *Inca* (actually *Inka*) denotes a high level of spiritual development. According to legend, at the end of the ceremony one of the candidates would visibly glow with brilliant light, as though the hand of Wiraccocha himself had selected the next Inca. This ability to shine is a sign of the sixth level of consciousness. Those who have visited great masters in India, such as Sai Baba, can confirm that highly evolved beings do seem to glow.

Some people believe that all eleven Inca rulers and their female counterparts, the *goyas*, had reached the sixth level of consciousness. As for the seventh level, this manifestation of consciousness is so far beyond anything we currently know, that it is difficult to even speculate about specific components.

Emergence of the Fifth Level of Consciousness and the Prospect of a Golden Age

Andean prophecy, like all myths and legends, is expressed in metaphoric language and cloaked in a specific worldview. The prophecy says that the rise once again of an Inca to the sixth level of consciousness indicates the emergence of a divine world leader capable of rebalancing world power. Then, and only then, will the golden age of humanity begin. This golden age, one also foretold by other prophecies around the world, is called the Taripay Pacha, the age of meeting ourselves again. It is, however, a potential, not a certainty.

There are various opinions about when this new age will begin. The Andean masters believe that the current *pachacuti* ended in August 1993,[19] a date that may mark the beginning of the sixth sun, or the sixth age. Other sources claim the sixth sun will begin in 2012, while Toltec *nagual* Miguel Ruiz says it occurred in January of 1992.[20] Interestingly the Q'ero adhere to an entirely different concept of world-ages, one that was superimposed on their culture by early Catholic clergy.[21]

Most Andean masters agree that there will be a transitional time until the emergence of the fifth level of consciousness among humanity as a whole. They believe the fifth level must manifest by 2012. It is prophesied that then the sixth level of consciousness will arise, and the new Sapa Inca will be recognized. Only then will the Taripay Pacha, the golden age of humanity, commence. The golden age will herald the beginning of the seventh sun, the time of fully awakened children of light.

To grasp the significance of how these levels of consciousness will manifest, it is critical to view each level as an opportunity for the collective elevation of consciousness. These are potentials that will manifest within a significant proportion of humanity, not just among a few individuals.

Moreover, the prophecy implies that all of humanity will attain the fifth level of consciousness simultaneously, that is, this golden age will be a collective experience of heightened consciousness. Although it says that the first of the twelve will emerge at the Festival of the Q'ollorit'i, the Festival of the Snow Star, this is not simply a reference to a physical event but to a collective readiness on the part of humanity. When enough human god-seeds are awake, free of fear and other negative aspects of the third and fourth levels of consciousness, the seed of the fifth level of consciousness can sprout within humanity as a whole.

Further, the prophecy relates that those who have achieved the fifth level of consciousness will come from all directions and from places sacred to the Inca. As discussed, it states that the first man will appear in the east, at the Festival of the Q'ollorit'i, and will walk to the south (Urcos), where the second will have appeared. They will then walk to the west (Cuzco) where the third will have appeared, and then to the north (Lima), where they will meet the first female. The cycle will then be repeated with the illuminated women, who will come from the north, south, east, and west. Thus the eight illuminated brothers and sisters will appear simultaneously, like the original eight Inca brothers and sisters, the first children of the light. These eight—four men (*malku's*) and four women (*nusta's*) will be joined by two more couples from the north, and then they will gather at the temple of Wiraccocha, which is light, the source of all creation. Finally, the prophecy states that the children of light will then dance in sacred ritual as fully conscious beings.

One interpretation of the prophecy is that these twelve individuals represent the collective awakened consciousness of humanity. Another possible interpretation is that the eight individuals represent the best of the remnant of the sacred seed of light originally planted here by the Elohim. The four coming from the north may also represent a new divine intervention, since in ancient Andean cosmology north was a reference to the Milky Way.[22] In this interpretation, the prophecy may mean that the evolving collective human consciousness will merge with a higher consciousness represented by four avatars, four brothers and sisters of light, from outside Earth's plane.

Moreover, the number twelve has many associations. It is possible that the twelve individuals mentioned in the prophecy may represent the twelve tribes of Israel, the twelve astrological signs, or the twelve tribes of the royal Incan lineage, the true children of light, the god-seeds planted here long ago on earth—the new Adam Kadmon.

The origins of the Festival of the Snow Star are themselves shrouded in mystery. Celebrated every year in May or June on the full moon, the festival is held high in the mountains, at an elevation of about 17,000 feet, at the foot of a huge glacier. This location is considered an ancient sacred site, but its true significance remains a mystery because the *quipus,* the knotted cords by which history was recorded, were destroyed. The legends tell of a magical appearance at this site of a Christlike young boy, who seemed to disappear into a rock located at the site in a blinding flash of light, allegedly leaving his image imprinted on the rock. This mystical appearance has been widely interpreted to foretell the messianic return of the Inca, the Children of the Sun.[23]

The Festival of the Snow Star coincides roughly with the ancient Festival of the Return of the Pleiades. Juan Nuñez del Prado says that the Pleiades, distinctly visible in the night sky, watches over the festival and serves as the *taqe* for the festival—a joiner of energy fields. He believes that the Pleiades emanates a powerful cosmic influence and that it serves to join diverse living energies together into a collective whole.[24]

In the coming golden age of humanity, the seed of the children of light will flower and humanity's higher consciousness will attract the great messengers of the gods, the condor and the hummingbird. We know that in Inca lore the condor is a symbol of the superior world. It is a guardian of the highest energy fields. The sacred hummingbird comes, according to legend, to dance above the heads of illuminated ones, to taste the sweet nectar of their enlightenment, and to pollinate the sacred flowers of the new consciousness. It is the divine messenger who carries the message of the illumination of humanity to the higher worlds. And from the flower of new human consciousness will come a new seed. In the distant future, from the new seed, a seventh level of consciousness may arise.

Now that a new consciousness appears to be unfolding, as Nuñez del Prado tells his students, it is now time for all of us who have bathed in the light of this sacred awakening to become *taqes,* joiners of energy fields. It is our task to help awaken our brothers and sisters.

5

AWAKENING

As we approach the millennium, there is much talk about the New Age. By some accounts the sixth sun, which marks the beginning of the sixth world-age, has already risen, and the much heralded astrological Age of Aquarius has arrived. However, there is confusion about when the Age of Aquarius actually begins because we are not certain when the Age of Pisces began. From an astrological perspective, an age is based on the concept of precession caused by the wobble in Earth's axis. A precessional period is approximately 2,160 years. Since the Age of Pisces began sometime between 144 B.C. and A.D. 496, the Age of Aquarius should either dawn soon or possibly closer to the middle of the 21st century.

The symbolism of these two ages reflects various forces operating in the world. The sign of Pisces is two parallel fish that point in opposite directions. Carl Jung has interpreted this symbol to mean two different forces. One fish, representing the first half of the cycle, symbolizes the pull toward spirit and the emergence of the Christ figure. The second, representing the second half of the cycle, symbolizes the pull toward matter and materialism.[1] The symbolism for the Age of Aquarius, the water bearer, represents our emergence from the unconscious state to a state of wholeness and integration.

Based on actual precession, the Age of Pisces concludes right around the end of the Mayan calendar. However, as we have seen, the ancient people of Mesoamerica and Peru marked their world ages a bit differently.

A great *pachacuti*, a time of great change, preceded each new world age. According to the Andean teachings, the initial part of the current *pachacuti* ended in August 1993. This was the first phase of the Taripay Pacha, "the time of meeting ourselves again." The second phase of the Taripay Pacha will bring the fifth and sixth level of consciousness. Both the fifth and sixth levels will manifest from the heightened consciousness of humanity as a whole. However, the emergence of these levels of consciousness depends on our awakening as individuals. The Andean masters say that this great transformation must occur by 2012. Of course, it is important to recognize that calendric references in myth and prophecy are not always to be taken literally. As we know, early cultures often used numbers symbolically and metaphorically.

It is no coincidence that the Mayan calendar ends in 2012 on December 21, the winter solstice. The current world-age, the fourth sun of the ancient Maya (the fifth sun of the Inca) is waning. The 5,125-year period that began in 3112 B.C. and marks the current cycle of seedings, is drawing to a close. The Maya predict that this cycle of time, their fourth sun, will end in great earthquakes—a notion that could be a metaphor for great cultural changes. However, it is important to remember that the simultaneous conjunction of the solstice sun with the galactic center offers a potential for great spiritual transformation and rebirth.

In this context, it is noteworthy that a very rare planetary alignment will occur on December 24, 2011, one year before the Maya calendar ends. On that date all the planets in our solar system will be spaced 30 degrees apart. Statistically, this phenomenon could only occur once every 45,200 years.[2] Apparently, the Maya foresaw this alignment and thus, to them, the year 2012 was far more than the end of a precessional cycle; it was a major galactic event.

Everywhere there are signs of *pachacuti*; great planetary changes are now abundant. Global weather patterns have become erratic, resulting in massive droughts, famines, hurricanes, and earthquakes. In addition, rain forests are burning at increasing rates, and the number of species on the planet is rapidly dwindling. Suggested causes include global warming, the depletion of the ozone layer, El Niño, La Niña, nuclear testing, sun spot activity, and the encroachment of technological civilization. Whatever the cause, it is clear our planet is undergoing massive changes.

Even so, *pachacuti* is likely to be a cultural, perceptual shift rather than a physical event.

Over 25 years ago, Frank Waters commented on the psychic parallels that accompany physical change. He postulated that the prevalence of worldwide revolutions; disruptions of economic, religious, and social values; and humankind's engrossing interest in UFOs were all indications of massive psychic changes that appear at the end of one precessional period and at the beginning of another.[3] In this regard, Jung said that changes in the constellation of psychic dominants, what he called the archetypes and what the ancients called gods, bring about or accompany long-lasting transformations of the collective unconscious.[4]

Interestingly, the psychic shift we are presently undergoing is being caused in part by our great technological advances and scientific breakthroughs, forcing us to rethink our worldview and pointing us in the direction of a more unified humanity. As a result, we are beginning to awaken to a new and more lucid experience of our reality.

Awakening the Human Hologram

Toltec *nagual* don Miguel Ruiz states that we entered the sixth sun on January 11, 1992, as the Aztec calendar predicted. He states that on that day the light coming from the sun changed. Don Miguel was in Teotihuacán with a group of his students and saw the color of the light actually change. According to him, the vibration and quality of the light shifted, becoming faster and more refined.[5] He believes this altered our DNA, not just for those at Teotihuacán on that day but for all of humanity, indeed for all life on the planet. He offers the following explanation:

> *DNA is a specific vibration of light that comes from the sun and becomes matter. Every kind of life on planet Earth, from the stones to the humans, has a specific vibration of light that comes from the sun. Each plant, animal, virus and bacterium has a specific ray of light. It is condensed by Mother Earth and the information carried in the light becomes matter. This reproduction is the method whereby silent knowledge is passed down from generation to generation of different life. DNA is specific to every form of life. Science has yet to differentiate the subtle distinctions in forms of DNA.[6]*

Revelations derived from particle physics research have also caused major changes in our perception of our world. Although the concept of light as a carrier of information is an ancient one, recent scientific developments indicate there may be a factual basis for this esoteric truth. The physics at work in holograms, for example, not only shows undisputedly that light both carries and "remembers" complex information but that it may be capable of transferring information instantaneously. The holographic model is one of the keys to understanding how the current planetary awakening is occurring, and, in this context, it is important to understand how holograms work.

Holograms are three-dimensional images produced by interference patterns. A hologram is created by sending a single beam of laser light through a beam-splitter, splitting the beam in two. One of the beams, called the reference beam, is passed through a special lens that spreads its rays into a wide beacon. Through the use of mirrors, the beacon is directed to a photographic plate. The second beam, called the working beam, is also passed through a lens and used to illuminate the object that is being photographed. When the two beams come together, their light waves interact, creating an interference pattern. When this pattern is captured on film, a hologram is created. Especially interesting is the fact that if you then shine a reference beam through the hologram you see the three-dimensional object that was originally recorded by the working beam. This happens, in some manner, because the working beam, the light that interacted with the object being photographed, maintained in its light waves a record of the object.

We used to believe absolutely that nothing could travel faster than the speed of light. We now believe that some things may go faster than light. There is as yet no experimental proof of this concept, but there is a theoretical basis. These theoretically faster-than-light particles are called tachyons. It is well known that electromagnetic waves, such as radio waves and X-rays, carry information that can be transferred at very rapid speeds of close to 186,000 miles per second. But more amazing is the fact that laser light is not only capable of retaining very complex patterns of information in the form of a hologram, it is conceivable that if a hologram was based on tachyon-like energy, it could transfer this information instantaneously, not limited to the speed of light.

Another exciting quality of the hologram is that every piece contains a blueprint of and can recreate the whole, making the implications of the hologram far reaching. At the very least the hologram and its potential gives a very helpful metaphoric basis for understanding creation. For example, the hologram may demonstrate that if the Elohim were indeed progenitors of the human species, somewhere within our DNA there is a code for the higher intelligence that represents divinity. The Bible states that humans were created in the image of God. The concept of the hologram tells us that if God is the master hologram, each human contains a blueprint of God—a blueprint that each of us can use to recreate an authentic and powerful vision of true Self.

Sensing Unbroken Wholeness

We may then consider every cell in the human body as a library of information. Each cell is made of molecules, each molecule is made of atoms, and atoms are made of electrons, neutrons, and protons. In connection with Einstein's familiar formula, $E=mc^2$, we have been taught that matter and energy are equivalent, that we can convert energy into matter, and that the energy in a piece of matter is equal to the mass of the matter times the speed of light squared. Thus, even minute amounts of matter represent a lot of energy. However, while in the past it was believed that electrons were particles—matter existing at some point in space—now, according to particle physics, electrons are not particles all of the time, but sometimes behave like waves of light. The current consensus is that they are both wave-like and particle-like, as is all matter. In fact, in the world of quantum physics, it seems these elementary "particles" (including electrons) don't really exist at all. What does exist are relationships, correlations, tendencies to actualize from a multifaceted set of potentials. A quantum physicist might say that electrons, like all other subatomic particles, are described by a "probability density state." At this level it is strikingly evident that there may be no objective physical reality at all. What the scientific community once thought was there in the sub-atomic realm and what the educated world was taught to perceive as real simply does not exist.

The new physics tells us that matter may actually be nothing more than a series of patterns out of focus and that subatomic "particles" aren't really made of energy, but simply *are* energy! The subatomic world of electrons, protons, and neutrons may thus be viewed as patterns of vibration within what Rupert Sheldrake calls a morphogenetic field, an organizing field that underlies a system's structure.[7]

We know we can convert matter into energy. We can burn wood and get heat. We can mathematically determine how much heat we would get from a pile of wood by using Einstein's formula. And the reverse is also true; energy can be converted into matter. For example, high-energy laser light can be observed to produce particle and anti-particle pairs. Cosmic rays, which are highly charged photons of light, have been observed to change form and become matter. Light, X-rays, and radio waves can all be converted back to particles. When their waves are slowed down they attain mass while retaining some wave-like characteristics.

Light also can either be considered a wave or a stream of particles. We know that photons carry energy, and that the amount of energy carried by a photon is proportional to the frequency of the light. That is, the higher the wave frequency, the more energy it carries. For example, X-rays and ultraviolet light have high frequency and high energy, while radio waves and infrared waves have low frequency and low energy.

Just as surprising as the apparent ethereal qualities of matter is the fact that it is the observer who brings the possibilities of the micro-world into existence. In experiment after experiment, it has been shown that when the observed function, the wave, interacts with the observing system, the person making the measurement, it changes to a new state. And whether what comes into actuality is a wave or a particle depends solely on the structure of the experiment. One interesting aspect of the apparent dual representative state of matter is that it is not a dual property of the particle, but rather a property of experimental observations. Niels Bohr, one of the founding fathers of quantum physics, pointed out that a particle only becomes a particle when someone is looking at it. The new physics tells us that the observer cannot observe anything without changing what he sees. Moreover, Princeton researchers Brenda J. Dunne and Robert G. Jahn have shown that this concept is not limited to the microworld of quantum interactions. Astonishingly, they have, through a series of well documented experiments, established that our minds, our intent, can alter the outcome of events.[8]

The implications of these findings are far reaching and significant for the world of everyday activity and human interaction. They imply that by our conscious intent we bring into manifestation what we want to perceive—that we can and do shape our reality.

In addition, according to new scientific thought, all matter and we ourselves consist of forms of light. In his book *Vibrational Medicine,* physician Richard Gerber actually describes all matter as "frozen light," light which has been slowed down and become solid. A quantum physicist would say that light in this context does not slow down—it always moves at the speed of light. Rather the light's photons get absorbed; its energy has been transferred. Gerber points out that atoms are primarily empty space. What fills them, he says, are packets of light that sometimes act as matter.[9]

If our bodies, at least metaphorically, are made of frozen light, they maintain the characteristics of light, which means they have frequency. Matter then may be thought of as light of a higher density. Thus, drawing on the implications of modern physics, we can conclude that human beings are made of light held in matter.

It is important to stress that Gerber's concept of matter as frozen light may not be merely metaphoric. Gerber describes the cellular matrix of the physical body as a complex energy interference pattern, interpenetrated by the organizing bioenergetic field of the etheric body. The physical body is therefore an energy field, and the field is made up of segments of vibration. As physicist Max Planck determined, higher frequency light means higher energy light. This concept also applies to what we think of as matter because we now know that all matter, not just quantum matter, also has frequency and thus waves—another scientific revelation that has radically changed the way we see the physical world. Using simple equations, Louis De Broglie discovered the wavelengths of waves that correspond to matter, which are not visible to us. Breakthroughs in quantum physics imply that all matter, including matter that makes up the human body, is itself made up of waves of light. It is therefore interesting to note that many ancient teachings saw humans as engendered by light, as children of light.

The Nobel Prize winning physicist David Bohm has written about what he calls the implicate order of the holographic universe. This concept suggests that the entire universe is an ever-changing cosmic hologram that is layered with information. Each layer holds a higher order of information and each higher order is enfolded in an aspect of space/time. The higher order may be thought of as consciousness that filters wave-like into form. Because it is a hologram, every segment contains information about the entire universe. Thus, consciousness is indeed in all things. Light is both the medium and the message.

Moreover, Bohm's work in quantum physics suggests that at the sub-atomic level all points in space are essentially the same, and therefore nothing is actually separate from anything else. This property is called non-locality. Bell's Theorem, developed a few years later by J. S. Bell, a Swiss physicist, provided mathematical proof of non-locality.[10] If we think about locality in terms of the particle behavior of light (a specific point in space), then non-locality can be seen in terms of light behaving as a wave (indistinguishable and interconnected).

What these concepts tell us is that, at the heart of our universe, there are no separate parts to anything, and that everything is connected to everything else. Moreover, they explain how information can be transferred superluminously, or faster than the speed of light. For example, if two photons are non-locally connected, communication between them can be instantaneous because they are not truly separate.

These discoveries from quantum physics have important implications for the evolution of human consciousness predicted by the Andean prophecies. As Bohm states, the world is an "unbroken wholeness"; everything is non-locally interconnected. We need to learn to perceive holistically because our world and the entire universe is actually interconnected. It is erroneous to continue to perceive our world as a conglomeration of separate, unrelated parts. In light of emergent scientific principles, the Cartesian world view is decidedly misleading.

Moreover, this holistic way of perceiving the world mirrors the teachings of ancient people such as the Inca. Wayu understood that she was nothing but energy, or light, and perceived everything around her as energy that vibrated at different frequencies. For her, all energy fields were intimately connected to each other. She could perceive frequencies of energy from many different sources—from the stars as well as from the sacred mountains. The universe was animated, and it communicated constantly with Wayu and everything else in the world. Information did not come to her in logically defined pieces (particle-like at the speed of light) but in an unbroken wholeness (at superluminal speed). She had access to the gateways of quantum potential. Buddhist and Hindu teachings have long told us that everything is energy dancing in form, and that the dance is a continuous weaving of the form and the formless. Now research from the frontiers of science is telling us the same thing.

The Unfolding of the Adam Kadmon

As discussed, laser light is focused, coherent light, in which every wave reinforces every action. Laser light is the most highly ordered, uniform structure found in nature. That is why it is brighter than ordinary light. Its separate waves seem to share an identity and therefore function as if they are one whole. As spiritual beings, we also can become coherent light once we have broken out of energy draining patterns and have learned how to use energy efficiently. As Carlos Castaneda said, we need to be impeccable with our energy.[11] That is, we need to give our best in everything we do, making optimal use of our individual energy. Only then can we vigilantly focus attention on our true essence as light-filled beings and develop our potential as god-seeds. We must avoid distraction of all types and stop wasting our precious energy. Functioning in a precise and focused way, like laser light, is the path to lucidity.

It seems clear that our hidden human potential is now unfolding. The higher order of consciousness that represents our next leap in human evolution is now being activated, and we are evolving into a higher frequency of light. A new light, known metaphorically as the sixth sun, is a catalyst. Its purpose is to release the hidden potential in the seed.

Moreover, it is possible that the hidden potential lies within the very fabric of our DNA. The human body may be a hologram, a reflection in the form of light encased in matter, of the greater cosmic hologram. Or, stated another way, the blueprint for humanity as a spiritual species, the Adam Kadmon, is holographically enfolded within us. We know that there are over 100 trillion cells in the human body, each of which has a complete set of DNA distributed in 23 chromosomes. Our DNA is a micro-universe set out in a continuous strand up to 6 feet long, with each strand having some 3 billion components. Scientists have found that most DNA components have no recognizable function within the current paradigm—only 3 percent are believed to be functional. It is possible that the other 97 percent known as junk DNA represents hidden human potential. What if they hold the code for the higher orders of human evolution that will be activated in the future?

Author Gregg Braden has theorized that the entire planet is undergoing a shift to a higher level of frequency, and that as a result, the currently unused portion of our DNA will be activated. He hypothesizes that due to exposure to more complex and shorter wavelengths of information, unique combinations of the amino acids that make up the DNA are capable of being produced. Braden believes that if human life is defined genetically by the type and arrangement of essential amino acids, and if these arrangements are changing, then a new life form is emerging (or at least capable of forming) from the human species.[12]

In this regard it is interesting to note that, as evolutionary biologist Elizabet Sahtouris points out, the history of evolution has repeatedly demonstrated that DNA is capable of rearranging itself intelligently in response to changing environmental conditions.[13] Therefore, some types of mutation may not be random at all. Our DNA may be capable of utilizing information and making conscious changes in its structure. That is, it may consciously direct the process of mutation, thus transforming a species.

This idea was recently discussed by Edgar Mitchell (the founder of the Noetic Sciences Institute) at a conference on science and consciousness. Mitchell referred to new unpublished but peer reviewed and verified research involving mutation in viruses conducted in Europe. This research appears to have established that DNA is capable of learning.[14]

Regardless of whether we are referring to a metaphoric concept or an actual possibility, it is interesting to speculate on what the origin of the "new light" might be. The current precessional cycle that began some 25,800 years ago is ending. For the first time in 25,800 years the December solstice sun will be conjuncting with the galactic center. Some people believe that, as a result, we are entering into a new cycle of communication with our galactic center, located 23,000 light years away in the heart of the Milky Way. If there is any truth to this notion, it is possible that the advent of a new precessional cycle will bring a shift in "light" and somehow catalyze a new potential for the human hologram.

According to the myth of the human god-seed, the seed will awaken when touched by a new light and begin to sprout. Legends of a return to paradise or a golden age are found worldwide. They are an aspect of most religions and include the concept of Shambala, the return of the great white brother, the golden age that is to follow the Kali Yuga foretold in Hindu teaching; the golden age prophesied by the Andean Masters; and the regeneration of earthly paradise promised in Judeo-Christian teachings. It seems apparent that this is the time foretold in many legends and myths from around the world and in the sacred traditions of many indigenous peoples—the time of the great awakening.

The God-seed Matures
The awakening of the god-seed may not be exactly what we expect. Our evolution as a species of light is just now beginning. If there were, as the Bible tells us, seven days of creation, we are now at the beginning of the seventh day. However, this is not a time of rest but a time of divine emergence. What is emerging is a profound awareness of the unbroken wholeness in which we live. In order to better understand this awakening, it is useful to use lucid dreaming as an analogy.

The practice of lucid dreaming (being conscious of one's own dream state) is a useful reference point. We all know that we dream during what is known as REM (rapid eye movement) sleep. However, most of us are not aware that we are dreaming. Only a few of us have the ability to realize we are dreaming during dreams. But as you become skilled at lucid dreaming, remaining fully conscious while your physical body is asleep, you can develop the ability to consciously direct dreams.

The process of awakening is very similar. You become fully conscious, fully lucid, awakening from the familiar everyday dream of ordinary waking consciousness to a new potential, directing your God-given energy with purpose and manifesting a sacred life on Earth. The word *lucid* comes from the Latin word, *lucere,* which means to shine and to be clear. Everything may be externally the same, but you are perceiving this world with a new and very clear vision, without limitation or any feelings of futility.

For most of us this is a slow process. We wake up a little, then fall back asleep. This happens over and over again. However, gradually our lucidity increases, and we eventually remain awake for longer periods. The ultimate goal is to remain fully awake in a state of lucidity all the time. This requires much effort, focus, and practice. True mastery requires that we shift our level of functioning, thus awakening the cosmic hologram hidden in all of us.

Emergence of a Species of Light

We have been taught that consciousness evolved through a gradual evolutionary process within the human form. Breakthroughs in new science suggest this perception may be inaccurate. We now understand that all biological life is self organizing and holistically ordered. The ancients understood that human consciousness came from a nonphysical reality. Consciousness, the higher order of expression, filtered wave-like into form. As we have seen, we are, in fact, beings of light, and as such, belong to a species of light. This is not just a metaphor but a physical reality.

It seems clear that a shift toward this awareness is occurring all around us. Through their writings, Gary Zukav (author of *The Dancing Wu Li Masters* and *The Seat of the Soul*) and others like Fritjof Capra, Fred Alan Wolf, Amit Goswami, and Deepak Chopra have helped us understand the implications of the new physics in relationship to the new consciousness that is emerging. Zukav believes that we have entered a new phase of evolution. Further, he also states that we are beings of light, and that the frequency of our light depends upon consciousness. Our thoughts and our emotions are also nothing but light, currents of energy at various frequencies. The key concept in much of the new science is that everything has frequency.

Andean teacher Juan Nuñez del Prado helps his students learn to distinguish between heavy, dense energies and refined energies. When we express negative emotions such as fear, hate, and anger, we are involved with dense energies and lower frequency currents. By contrast, when we express more positive emotions like love and kindness, we are dealing with more refined energies and higher frequency currents. The lower the frequency, the less consciousness and light; the higher the frequency, the more consciousness and light. It makes perfect sense that as we express more of our true divine natures, the energy we create is more refined.

In our universe all physical light is a reflection of nonphysical light originating from pure consciousness that preceded and gave rise to form. Thus, although we exist in the physical form, we are a reflection of the divine light of a higher order. Because the ancients understood the potency of divine reflection and that the light of consciousness is not limited to the laws of the physical universe, their ceremonial sites were built to reflect both inner light and divine consciousness.

Gary Zukav believes that we are evolving from one frequency spectrum to another. As humans we perceive a specific color spectrum and our five basic senses function within a limited range; yet we also know invisible rays of light border the limited spectrum we see, and that higher and lower frequencies of light exist than we can perceive with the five senses. Nonphysical light also has a frequency range. We exist at a certain level of consciousness, a certain frequency of light, but we may now be making a jump to a higher frequency spectrum of light—light far more refined.

We often associate more refined energies and light qualities with spiritually evolved beings, such as great world teachers like Jesus and Mohammed. They represent the fully empowered human seed whose role is to show us what we will become. However, to many, this potential has seemed unattainable on Earth. It is critical at this point in the evolution of our collective human consciousness that we understand that it is not unattainable and come forward to claim our true identity and divine potential. The god-seed in each one of us is already invested with divine energy, the same potential that was realized by mythical god-men of the past.

The awakening process requires that we begin to function as beings of light. As Zukav reminds us, we are dynamic beings of light capable of regulating the energy that flows through our systems with our thoughts and intents:

> The Light that flows through your system is Universal energy. It is the Light of the Universe. You give that Light form. What you feel, what you think, how you behave, what you value and how you live your life reflect the way you are shaping the light that is flowing through you. They are thought forms, the feeling forms and the outer forms that you have given to Light. They reflect the configuration of your personality, your space-time being.[15]

When you become integrated with the light that flows through your system, as Zukav says, you become like laser light, coherent, a beam of light in which every wave precisely reinforces every other wave. The integrated human, the god-seed, is a being of laser light.

Understanding Light Dynamics

God-seeds act with focused, conscious intent. They understand light dynamics, realizing that each thought and each emotion they experience sets light in motion. They take responsibility for the light that flows through them, aware that they have chosen to bring this light to Earth.

As god-seeds mature, they become more and more luminous, eventually becoming illuminated ones. They develop the ability to pull in higher frequencies of light and to radiate these into the world. They heal, teach, and serve where needed, making their light available to individuals and to world situations that can benefit from healing. They understand that they are merely servants of the light, here to assist the planet and its inhabitants in achieving and maintaining a higher level of functioning.

God-seeds comprehend the fundamental truth that has been verified by quantum physics—that light is responsive to intent. Quantum physics has shown that the nature of light as we perceive it depends solely on the intention of the perceiver, since whether light takes the form of a wave or a particle depends on the intent of the observer. The same rules apply to inner light, whose form of manifestation depends on the intent of the human shaping it. We need to be fully conscious of how we use our intent. This is what it means to be awake.

The conscious use of intent is the key to the next leap in human evolution. To grasp the meaning of this, we need to realize that our true human potential has not yet been developed due to the devastating consequences of our individual and collective false perceptions. We must act knowing that our intentions create the world, rather than feeling like we are being acted upon by outside forces beyond our control.

Because matter is light frozen in form, we have within us the wavelike nature of pure light. The new physics tells us that at a subatomic level the physical vehicle that forms our body looks, feels, and acts like physical light. The light that informs our consciousness is nonphysical light. Both aspects of the light that fills our being have distinct internal orders, but they are governed by a higher order that may not be limited by the physical laws of this space/time. The human hologram is therefore a dynamic form capable of endless expansion.

We have been brought up to believe many false concepts about ourselves, some of which come from Newtonian physics and the Cartesian worldview. There is nothing inherently wrong with these systems of thought; they have just been overapplied. They cannot describe all aspects of reality. Many other falsehoods we live with come from our conventional religious systems. For example, the Judeo-Christian tradition gives us the story of the Garden of Eden, a myth that unfortunately has been misinterpreted and causes great harm to our collective psyche. It is possible we were never banished from the garden, and we did not sin. Thus, we are not unworthy spiritually.

How human experience came into existence can also be explained in terms of light descending deeper into matter and becoming frozen in form—the natural process of involution that preceded the evolutionary period that is now approaching. This was a necessary phase of the process of light interpenetrating the denser realms of the physical aspect of creation. Creation, in this context, did not end in 6 days, but is an ongoing process. We are being created "into the form and similitude of God" right now.

With the advent of higher consciousness, the light that has been hidden in form is awakening to its potential. We are now shifting from a frozen involutionary process into a dynamic evolutionary process. As human god-seeds, our light is rising upward just as the sprout rises and reaches to the light. As we reach upward, we pull ourselves from the lower frequency of matter to higher, more refined realms. As we become fully conscious, we will raise all matter to a higher frequency, literally infusing all matter with higher vibrations of light.

This is why we are here and why light entered matter. There never has been any separation. The ancient people of Mesoamerica and Peru knew who they were, believing that their ancestors came from the stars and that they were children of light. We forgot who we are, falling asleep in the dark and potent realms of matter. Now, with the birth of the sixth sun, we are beginning to collectively awaken. The children of light are returning.

6

LIBRARIES OF ANTIQUITY

THERE ARE MANY TOOLS AVAILABLE TO HELP THE HUMAN god-seed awaken, and sacred sites around the world are some of the most powerful.

When asked about the power of sacred sites, H. H. the Dalai Lama once stated that a place becomes holy by the power of the individual spiritual practitioner who lives there, that the power of an individual's spirit "charges" the place. The residual energy at a sacred site can then charge anyone who visits the site.[1] Anyone who has visited a sacred site can verify the validity of H. H. the Dalai Lama's statement.

There are sacred sites all over the world. Stonehenge, Mecca, Iona, Haleakala, the Ganges, Delphi, Palenque, Jerusalem, the Egyptian pyramids, Chartres, Chaco Canyon, Teotihuacán, and Machu Picchu are but a few, and people are visiting such sites in astonishing numbers. For example, according to the English Tourist Board, over 70 percent of the people who visit England come expressly to visit the cathedrals, shrines, and sacred sites that dot the countryside.[2] Each year more than a half a million people journey to the desolate landscape of Australia to visit Ayres Rock (another sacred site).

A Network of Sacred Sites

There is no question that individuals can, as H. H. the Dalai Lama suggests, charge physical space with higher vibrational energy, and that sacred sites are profoundly spiritual places. However, there are also unique physical characteristics associated with sacred sites. Many of the sacred sites on this planet are thought to be connected by an almost invisible grid of astronomical and geometrical lines. Russian scientists have found evidence of a faint pattern of magnetic lines running around our planet that make the shape of a dodecahedron (a 12-sided figure) imposed on an icosahedron (a 20-sided figure).[3] It has been speculated by some researchers that this is evidence that the planet was once a large crystal or that it was energized in some manner by a crystalline core.[4] Scientists studying this phenomenon have found that the locations of the most ancient civilizations and their sacred sites occur along the magnetic lines of this planetary icosahedron.[5]

Meteorological and geological maps have established that maximal and minimal atmospheric pressure areas are found precisely at the nodes of the dodecahedron. These nodes are the areas where hurricanes originate and where the oceans have huge vortices of current. Core faults as well as unusual features like the Bermuda Triangle also occur on the nodes.[6] Rudolph Steiner, the founder of a field of study called anthroposophy, has said that as a living entity Earth would energetically take the form of a dodecahedron-icosahedron,[7] a statement that correlates with the findings of Buckminster Fuller.[8] Another Russian, Vitaly Kabachenko, who studied maps of the Earth taken from outer space, found that they showed a grid barely noticeable as black streaks on the ocean floor and in the sky.[9] Others, including Aimee Michell, a French writer who has written about the UFO phenomenon, have said that UFO sitings tend to occur along similar magnetic lines that also form a planetary grid.[10] Moreover, increasing numbers of people believe that Earth is a living organism and that its body is intersected with *ley*, (energy) lines that function just like the acupuncture meridians found in the human body. It may be appropriate to think of such a grid as the energy body of the earth.

There has been much speculation about the origins of such grids. After reviewing evidence found on many ancient maps, geomancer and author John Michell concluded that in our prehistory someone, or some group, precisely mapped the entire globe and laid out a network of astronomical and geometrical lines that cross the entire planet. According to Michell, many of the most sacred sites are found on these lines, including sites made of vast blocks of stone that function as massive astrological instruments. He has concluded that the human predecessors who built these sites had to have had advanced technologies and "remarkable powers."[11]

Not surprisingly, Teotihuacán and many of the other ancient sites of Mesoamerica and Peru are found along these grids. Apparently, based upon their experiences, the ancients of these regions and elsewhere believed that the planetary energy lines had powers related to healing and the expansion of consciousness.

Aspects of Sacred Space

There are numerous theories regarding sacred space. Sig Lowgren, a dowser who has studied many sacred sites around the world, believes that most of these sacred sites were located and designed to enhance contact with spiritual realms. He has suggested that through the use of sacred geometry a physical space that has the right characteristics could actually be tuned like a musical instrument so it could resonate at a specific frequency. After dowsing a number of sacred sites, he has found that most of them are places where yin and yang energies within the earth converge. The yin, feminine-receptive energy, is found where there are domes and veins of underground water, while the yang, or masculine force, is carried by straight beams of energy or *ley* lines.[12]

We know that certain people (dowsers) have the ability to sense underground water and magnetic and telluric forces. In regions where water is scarce, the use of dowsers is a common and relatively reliable practice. Research has shown that dowsers respond to electrostatic charges and to changes in the electromagnetic gradient above the ground. The charges are caused by the electric currents of flowing subterranean water. Subsequent research has shown that the magnetic sensors in the human body are located in the pineal gland,[13] which implies that theoretically, everyone has the ability to sense such currents.

Lowgren has found that the energies measurable at sacred sites vary throughout the calendar year. We know that many of our ancient sites were designed for use on solstices, equinoxes, and other specific dates. For example, Stonehenge is associated with the summer solstice sunrise. New

Grange is associated with the winter solstice sunrise. The most powerful time to be on the Pyramid of the Sun at Teotihuacán is at high noon. Few things could be more dramatic than the spectacular effect caused by the sun lighting the crown chakra of Wiraccocha at the solstice in Ollantaytambo or the solstice sun as it penetrates the sungate at Machu Picchu.

Lowgren also discovered that when an energy *ley* line aligns with the rising and setting of the sun, the *ley* line actually becomes more potent. After measuring the energy present during such critical alignments, he was able to determine that at these times the energy alignments increase the energy available at a power center. It is clear that the designers of such sacred places were aware of these special energy dynamics, and that the sites were designed to maximize the daily and seasonal energy intensifications.[14]

Ritual sites also employ sacred geometry—the geometry found in nature and consisting of the sets of correspondences, geometrically expressed by ratios. Paul Devereux, the editor of *Ley Hunter* magazine and the director of the Dragon Project that studied the energy effects of sacred sites, states that sacred, or canonical, geometry is not an obscure, archaic invention but an extrapolation by humankind of the patterns in nature that frame the entry of energy into our space/time dimension. It is the geometry found in the formation of matter at the subatomic level, in the natural motions of astronomical phenomena of the universe, and in organic forms of plant life. In brief, sacred geometry shows us the blueprint of all creation.[15]

Encoded into many sites are the sacred geometric ratios of creation, which reflect the ancient law of correspondence—as above, so below. Through the principles of sacred geometry, ancient sites functioned as tools for integrating the different dimensions, accessing the various frequency spectrums found in the universe.

For example, the entire Sacred Valley of the Inca is a masterpiece of sacred geometry. And the spectacular architecture of the early Maya and Olmec people, used for initiations and for ecstatic rituals, was interlaced with energetic gateways to the higher dimensions. The people of these regions both embodied and enacted the principles of sacred correspondence.

In addition, there are other aspects of correspondence that may be relevant to sacred sites, such as the principle of harmonic resonance. When two objects resonate in a harmonic state, energy is exchanged between them, which may be relevant to the energy dynamics that exist at some of the sacred places on our planet. Correspondence can be a function of form, as in sacred geometry; it can also be a function of vibration, as in harmonic resonance.

Research done at sacred sites has also shown that the sites themselves often contain unusual amounts of natural radioactivity and magnetic anomalies. When members of the Dragon Project extensively studied ancient sites in the British Isles, they found that certain sites had magnetic anomalies, while other sites contained radioactive rocks.[16] Although research of such sites has been inconclusive, they nevertheless remain of interest to researchers because so many people report having unusual experiences at such places. It is not uncommon for visitors to experience transcendent feelings, visions, insights, and paranormal occurrences—all reasons why such places are sought out by so many people.[17]

Teotihuacán and the Speed of Light

The sacred sites of our world share one fundamental characteristic—they are all places where spirit communicates. For some that communication takes the form of heightened awareness, while others experience archetypal imagery or altered states—all encounters with the divine.

Virtually all of the ceremonial centers in Mesoamerica and Peru—including Teotihuacán, Machu Pichu, Palenque, and Monte Albán—were built for the express purpose of divine communication although we do not know the specifics of how these sites were used or their purpose in a larger world context. Perhaps, as John Michell suggests, they are part of a larger complex of structures that ring the planet, a type of tuning fork that was deliberately built by divine beings, or perhaps arose independently from a collective impulse. Whatever the origin of sacred sites, it is clear that their builders knew a lot more than we do about the subtle characteristics of energy and that they had precise knowledge of astronomical events.

Many of the ruins of antiquity like the Great Pyramid and Stonehenge were designed as astronomical and geodetic markers that theoretically aligned our world with the greater cosmic whole. In 1972, an American engineer, Hugh Harleston, Jr., began to study the ruins at Teotihuacán and found evidence that the Pyramid of the Sun was designed to function as an equinoctial clock just like the Great Pyramid.[18] He also uncovered evidence that Teotihuacán, Palenque, the Great Pyramid, and Solomon's Temple were all based on the same sacred number system. Further, he found that the entire Teotihuacán complex was laid out as a massive calendric system and that its builders not only had knowledge of π (pi) but of many other mathematically abstract relationships that are the basis of the universe. Through precise measurements of angles at the site, Harleson showed that universal constants that the rest of world did not discover until centuries later, including the speed of light, were incorporated into the design of Teotihuacán.[19]

The speed of light, first measured by French physicist Claus Roemer in 1849, and later refined by Jean Foucault as 186,282 miles per second, remains constant under all conditions. Even if you are moving at an incredible speed toward a source of light, it will still take the same amount of time for the light to reach you as when you are stationary. To explain this apparent anomaly, Einstein developed the Theory of Relativity, which states that time and distance actually change to accommodate the universal constant, the speed of light. It is indeed bewildering how the ancients could have known about something this abstract. They were obviously either far more scientifically advanced than we imagine, or they had unexplained abilities—possibly the capability of perceiving in a holographic manner. They may also have had access to sacred knowledge that they perceived in a manner beyond the boundaries of our five senses.

Another intriguing question is why they would have encoded abstract information like the speed of light into their architecture. One possibility is that they did so to show later descendants who they were, having realized that future advanced civilizations would have knowledge of universal constants. Perhaps they left clues about these constants to help us awaken to our cosmic history.

In any case they left behind megalithic structures like Teotihuacán which incorporated coded information. And with their complex, precise calendar system, they could foresee cycles of time. They could have foreseen, for instance, that a time of great darkness was coming and that in the near future the remnant seed would fall further into matter. Such clues may tell us that the builders of Teotihuacán were an early incarnation of the children of light, the offspring of the great Elohim. It is entirely possible that they left encoded in stone a record of the sacred history of light, tools that would help future generations determine their heritage.

Doorways of Harmonic Frequency

Don Miguel Ruiz has arrived at his own theory of Teotihuacán, based on reading the historic record left in the stone itself. Ruiz comes from a lineage of *naguals* that can be traced back to the ancient Toltecs. His grandfather told him that the ruins held great power and cautioned that he should not enter them until he was ready. In 1988, he made his first visit to Teotihuacán, where he was flooded with ancient memories. As he sat on the Pyramid of the Sun, he was able to attune to the frequency of the stone itself and to see in his mind's eye what had been recorded energetically during the time the culture of Teotihuacán was at its zenith. Through a series of visions, don Miguel Ruiz came to understand how Teotihuacán was used as an initiation chamber and how it was and still is "the place where man becomes god." He believes the site itself is a powerful field of highly charged energy where one can, through a series of ritual practices, find the path to divinity, to freedom.[20]

There is no doubt that the heightened energy experienced at such sites is perceptible and tangible. It vibrates through our chakra systems and energy bodies. Although the stones that make up such sites appear to be visibly solid, we know that they are energy fields and that all matter has frequency—at least at the subatomic level. We now know that at a subatomic level what we perceive of as matter may simply be bands of vibration bound within a field, and that although most of these frequencies are too minimal for us to measure, they are not necessarily too small for us to perceive.

Until recently no one was able to measure the frequency of a human energy field. The first individual to do so was Valerie Hunt, a physical therapist and professor of kinesiology at UCLA, who found that an electromyograph, used to measure the electrical activity of muscles, could also measure the human energy field. She discovered that the average frequency in the human body is between 0 to 30 cycles per second (cps), while electrical activity in the brain is between 0 and 100 cps, and muscle frequency can increase to 225 cps. Interestingly, she also found that another frequency field emanates from the body with frequencies that are considerably higher, generally ranging between 100 and 1600 cps. This field is strongest in the parts of the body associated with the chakras.

One of the most fascinating aspects of Hunt's findings is that the frequencies associated with a person's consciousness can be measured. She discovered that individuals who focus their attention and energy primarily on the material world have frequencies in the range of around 250 cps, not far from the physical body's own range, while people who are consistently psychic demonstrate frequencies between 400 and 800 cps. Individuals in trance or channeling have even higher frequencies, between 800 and 900 cps. Hunt considers those who have frequencies of 900 cps and over to be mystical personalities. Using a modified electromyogram that can detect higher frequencies, Hunt claims to have measured frequencies up to 200,000 cps in the energy fields of some individuals.[21]

When the energy of a space is "charged" by an individual of high frequency, as H. H. the Dalai Lama suggests, the frequency of the energy field itself attains a very high vibration. There are numerous such "charged" places, including the caves of Arunacula and the ashrams of the great saints of India, the Temple of Wiraccocha, Machu Picchu, Palenque's Palace of Inscriptions, the Palace of the Butterflys at Teotihuacán, and sacred tombs throughout the world.

The concept of harmonic resonance tells us that energy can be exchanged between two objects in a relationship. We know that energy, such as radio waves and other forms of light radiation can carry information. Therefore ruins such as Teotihuacán may function as libraries which, when opened energetically, reveal their secrets to individuals whose consciousness is receptive. Perhaps don Miguel Ruiz was able to perceive the information encoded at Teotihuacán because his energy body was in harmonic resonance with the frequency at Teotihuacán.

Sacred Sites and Altered States

Dragon Project director Paul Devereux suggests that sacred sites were not intended to be used in a normal state of consciousness but in altered states, which can be induced in many ways, such as through drumming, ritual, prayer, and dreaming, as well as mind-altering drugs.[22] Moreover, the energy fields of the sites themselves often promote such altered states or perceptual shifts. In the *nagual* tradition, such states can occur following the process of "stopping the internal dialogue." We cannot begin to access the more subtle vibrations in our environment until our receptive abilities are focused and our mind is devoid of chatter and biased opinions that are common aspects of ordinary consciousness. Thus sacred spaces should be entered in a state of inner quiet and nonjudgmental receptivity to facilitate communication with the energy present. If we have developed focused awareness, we will be able to broaden our perceptual abilities.

People who have experienced having their attention shifted through the energy in a sacred space often describe resonating at a higher frequency and experiencing a state of heightened awareness. Perspective shifts and becomes more transpersonal. The *nagual* tradition calls this "having your assemblage point shifted." From this "shifted" perspective, the world does not consist of matter or separate objects; instead, everything is perceived as energy fields that cluster in different bands, not unlike the findings of the new physics. Don Juan Mateus, Carlos Castaneda's teacher, said there are some 48 energy bands in our universe of which seven might be perceptible, but only two can be perceived through ordinary perception. Within a given band only certain emanations, or frequencies, are aligned at a given time. This alignment is the basis of our perception. Our assemblage point determines which emanations are aligned in a given moment of perception. A shift in the assemblage point will result in alignments within the band of emanations normally not perceived.[23]

In the *nagual* system of perception popularized by Carlos Castaneda, there exist three forms of attention or levels of awareness, determined by how the energy emanations that give order to a perception are selected. The first attention, which is culturally conditioned, orders the field of perception in which our ordinary lives take place, the known world we perceive with the five senses. The second attention orders the world of the unknown. The third attention integrates the first two attentions, enabling us to access that which is otherwise unknowable.[24]

The fields of energy that surround us are selectively organized by the first attention. This makes our reality generally consistent and predictable. The implication of this imposed selective level of organization is that our reality is actually consensual (something we all agree on). If this inner structuring is somehow disrupted, our perception of the world "collapses" and our "world is stopped."[25]

The *nagual* understanding of the attentions has been validated by neu-rophysiological research. This research has shown that visual information perceived by our eyes is first sent to our temporal lobe, where it is edited, and the edited version is received by the visual cortex. Some studies indi-cate that less than half of what we "see" is based on information that actu-ally entered our eyes, which means that the brain pieces together most perception from our expectations of what the world should look like based on past experience, filtering out the rest.[26] When we are able to shift to an altered state of perception, or "stop the world," it may be possible to cir-cumvent this filtering mechanism.

Irrespective of the mechanisms that determine our perception, indi-viduals often experience aspects of nonordinary reality when they visit sacred sites, something that has been well documented by many people, including author James Swan. Swan reports that it is not unusual for peo-ple to experience ecstasy, visions of mystical beings, feelings of unification with nature, vivid dreams, interspecies communications, the hearing of voices, death and rebirth, and similar supernatural states.[27] It is entirely possible that the codings imprinted in sacred sites automatically shift the assemblage points of people at the site.

Understanding Sacred Correspondence

We know that the people of Mesoamerica and Peru built and used sacred sites primarily for ceremonial purposes. As we have seen, there is sub-stantial evidence that they were built to awaken higher states of con-sciousness and to create opportunities for divine communication. After flourishing, the ceremonial areas of these regions were abandoned. Prior to abandoning these sites, it is likely that our predecessors deliberately sealed certain critical features of the sites energetically as a form of pro-tection. Since they knew a time of darkness was coming, they may have realized that as the human god-seed descended further into the world of matter, it would lose the ability to function in the higher dimensions, and thus they locked the portals within these sacred libraries of divine consciousness. They probably knew that the power hidden within the sacred sites themselves would help to catalyze the future awakening of the seed.

There is a simple but ancient formula for accessing this hidden power, a key well known by the builders—the law of sacred correspondence, the principle of "as above, so below." Basically, the power of these sites can be accessed at any time when the light that shines from below is equal to the light that shines from above. In our space/time, this means that to access this power our own personal light must reflect the higher light, our frequency must resonate with a higher harmonic, thus assuring that access to such power is never given to those who are spiritually unprepared.

In this context, it is important to remember that all living things emit light. We do not normally perceive this light because it is beyond our spectrum and filtered out by the brain. Fritz Albert Popp, the German scientist who discovered this effect, believes DNA is the source of this light, which ranges from ultraviolet to infrared.[28] Eastern teachings tell us that the living light is encoded in our form. The ancient concept of the macrocosm as microcosm also tells us that the greater divine life (light) is reflected in the human body. Expressed in another manner, this means that the Adam Kadmon, the spiritual human created "in the image and likeness" of the Elohim, has encoded within it a divine blueprint. Through knowledge of the science of vibration, we can learn to unlock these mysteries. This is how the Adam Kadmon (the light body) unfolds from the implicate order.

Teachers don Miguel Ruiz, Juan Nuñez del Prado, and Alberto Villoldo, all of whom work with the energies of the ancient sites, help apprentices purify their light bodies (their energy fields) so they may access higher light fields. They understand that it is the physical body that must be attuned to the higher light vibrations. All teach various processes for aligning the human body with higher vibrational energies to provide access to the superior worlds.

Juan Nuñez del Prado teaches his students to become aware of the subtle characteristics of energy, to sense higher and lower vibrational qualities. He uses the power inherent in the ancient Incan sites to help his students cleanse and strengthen their light bodies and teaches them how to work energetically with such power, pulling in higher vibrational energies and releasing denser energies. He considers the ancient sites energetic openings to the world of refined energies.[29]

In his books, Villoldo describes the methods his teachers, Antonio Morales and Eduardo Calderon, used in working with him at Machu Picchu and other sites to awaken him to shamanic and spiritual powers. He incorporates those methods into the Incan Medicine Wheel he teaches.

Don Miguel Ruiz uses the power of Teotihuacán and other Mesoamerican and Peruvian sites to help his apprentices shift their assemblage points and awaken from the "dream" of ordinary reality, the first attention. Through the *nagual* practice of stalking, he teaches his apprentices to cleanse their energy bodies of emotional debris and patterns that no longer serve them. Another *nagual* practice taught by don Miguel Ruiz is dreaming, the practice of exploring nonordinary reality. This process does not use rational, cognitive thinking but does use the full potential of imagination to break the hold of the rational mind on our thought processes—allowing a more expansive spectrum of reality and shifting our vibration.

The Elevation of Collective Consciousness

We are approaching an unprecedented time in the development of human consciousness when the sixth sun will catalyze a new human evolution. Never has it been more important for us to awaken to our cosmic origins. We desperately need to break out of the box that limits our perception of our potential. Our narrow attitudes, sensory limitations, fears of the unknown, and forgetfulness have trapped us for far too long. Fortunately, the libraries of antiquity left to us by our forebears offer us a way to remember who we are. When we approach these libraries with receptivity and in a spirit of gratitude, they will reveal their secrets.

As we have discussed, it is possible that ancient ceremonial sites were part of a giant grid of energy that surrounds the planet. We know they were built by highly advanced individuals, perhaps the Elohim, who had a galactic awareness that we are just beginning to comprehend.

If such a grid exists, what will occur when it becomes activated? José Argüelles tells us we are now in the time of the great galactic synchronization that will result in the quickening and transformation of matter. Based on the Mayan calendar, this transformation coincides with Baktun 12, which began in 1618 and will end in 2012.

Moreover, he believes that various releases of nuclear energy since 1945 have affected the vibratory structure of Earth itself. To compensate for this vibrational shift, he predicts that the crystalline core of Earth will make an adjustment in the form of a series of waves until a new level of harmonic resonance is reached, resulting in a vibratory shift in the planetary light body itself.[30] Argüelles explains that this is our galactic destiny, part of the development of a fully conscious planetary light body.

> *Here is the picture of what has been happening. Slowly, over the eons, at Earth's core, the iron crystal lodestone of her [the Earth's] harmonic gyroscope has been emitting the resonant frequencies that keep her in orbit. These resonate frequencies have a particular shape or form, for form follows frequency. This is why Plato described the Earth as being like a leather ball sewn together from twelve different pieces, creating a dodecahedron or twelve interfaced pentagons. The vertices between the pentagonal pieces define the structure of the resonate body of the Earth as the frequency emissions reach the surface.*

> *As the core resonance continuously emanates out to the surface of the Earth and beyond, an etheric grid comes into being, forming the foundations of the planetary light body. Attuned through the frequency patterns of the DNA infrastructure, animal migration patterns and human settlements tend to conform to the lines and nodal points of the grid. Of course, the grid is warped and reshaped by tectonic plate activity, variable shifts in terrain and atmosphere, and solar-galactic triggered fluctuations in the electromagnetic field of the planet itself. Nonetheless, anchored at the poles, amplified at times by (to us) unforeseen and imperceptible shifts in the galactic program, the continuous pulsation of the grid slowly shapes the infrastructure of the planetary light body.[31]*

To counterbalance the effect of increased technology and the impulse toward materialism, the resonant frequency of Earth's core has intensified, a phenomenon that, as Argüelles explains, is part of the synchronization of the frequency of Earth with the larger galactic whole.

What this may look like from the human perspective is a gradual shift in consciousness to an understanding of a new worldview. This new worldview will make it evident that the world we live in is a living entity, and that it is part of a larger whole. We will be able to perceive that all matter is energy, that we are wave-like, that we are in constant communication with the whole. Through this shift in consciousness, we will begin to function as multi-dimensional beings, and we will realize we have potentials beyond anything yet dreamed of, adding our heightened light vibration to the Earth's own.

As these new human potentials begin to unfold we will fully grasp that we are indeed god-seeds. As god-seeds we have the power of conscious intent. We can learn to bring potential into form. Our DNA is specially programmed, encoded with light-sensitive patterns that will unfold the new humans we are evolving into. This new human is a being of light, capable of functioning with a fully activated light body.

In order to unlock the potentials in our DNA, we need to start perceiving ourselves as beings of light and understand how to use conscious intent. From this viewpoint of higher consciousness, we are akin to electrons in our own molecules, which exhibit their potential when we perceive them as waves or as particles.

As we begin to develop our potentials as human god-seeds, we will fulfill prophecies about the return of the light. The spirit of Quetzalcoatl, the Christ, the Pahana, the Great White Brother, the Illuminated Ones, the Capac Inca will return and again walk among us. The boundaries of the black box of limited perception and limited potential will dissolve. The Newtonian-Cartesian perspectives that shape our current worldview will be relegated to a more appropriate role, continuing to be an important tool in defining ordinary reality but no longer limiting our perception of nonordinary realities to which we have access. In time, our overreliance on these concepts may come to be viewed as little more than a strange aberration that occurred briefly within human history.

Many people believe that the activation of the grid, the planetary light body, is already occurring, awakening our potentials. As we individually awaken to the light within human form, the light within the planetary form is simultaneously awakening. This is occurring because within the larger whole, a new pattern is emerging—the universe is holographic.

Science has long told us that one of the rules of the universe is that things always tend toward a greater state of disorder. However, chemist Ilya Prigogine received a Nobel Prize for unraveling the mystery of "dissipative structures" which indicate that, on the contrary, from apparent disorder, new and more complex systems can suddenly appear. He believes that these layers of complexity are always there, implicit in the higher order of the universe itself.[31] It seems clear that a new structure is now unfolding within both the planetary and human psyches. This new level of complexity will give us a radically new perspective of ourselves in relation to the whole.

The great and ancient ceremonial centers that ring our planet can be tools in service of the new alignment. Some people believe that these centers were built by master builders specifically to help us align to the new, higher order of being. The Andean prophecies tell us that the sixth level of consciousness will emerge when we return to the vibrational level that is still held at ancient ceremonial centers like the Temple of Wiraccocha. The new consciousness will emerge when we as a human community collectively align our vibration with the higher vibration that is awakening within the planetary light field. The doorways to divine consciousness, the ancient gateways, which are in actuality the next level of the implicate order, will open when "the light that comes from below is equal to the light that comes from above."

7

STEPPING INTO
THE ANGEL LIGHT

AMANUMURU IS A LEGENDARY PERUVIAN GOD-MAN WHO
one day walked through an ancient doorway and returned to his celestial
home. It is said that, like Wiraccocha, he returned to the ocean from which
he came. In Quechua *amanu* means snakelike living energy. The eminent
esotericist Manly B. Hall has equated the legendary Amanumuru of Peru
with Quetzalcoatl of Mesoamerica, pointing out that Amarcuca translates
as "the land of the plumed serpent." In addition, he implies that Amarcuca
is the origin of the word *America*. Hall believes that in the early history of
the Americas the priests of this "god of peace" ruled both hemispheres of
this world.[1]

The Central Sun and the Story of the Golden Disk

According to legend, when Amanumuru came to this world, he brought
with him the famous golden disk, which hung in the great Temple of the
Sun in Cuzco before the decline of the Inca. Today it is still possible to see
the holes through which the ropes passed that held the disk at the Convent
of Santo Domingo, which is known to be built upon the Incan Temple of
the Sun. The disk is said to have remained at the Temple of the Sun until
word arrived of the landing of Pizarro. It was then removed and hidden in

Lake Titicaca. The prophecy says that someday the golden disk will be returned to the Temple of the Sun.

The disk was said to have originated outside of this space/time and was brought from Lemuria, the Land of Mu, with Amanumuru when he fled the sinking continent. Whatever its origin, the disk is not a representation of our solar sun but of the great central sun, the creative force the ancients called the Mother Sun. It is said that through certain vibrations the disk could cause great earthquakes and even change the rotation of Earth itself. Further, it could allegedly attune to a person's frequency pattern and transport that person wherever he wanted to go, merely by the mental picture he created.[2]

In addition to the reputed powers of the historic disk, it is also a metaphor for the potential of higher consciousness. There is a golden disk within each of us. We are not only illuminated by the external sun; we are illuminated by the light that shines from within.

The external light that fills our world comes from the sun, the center of our solar system. Our sun is an average-sized yellow star at the very fringe of the Milky Way, about 93 million miles away and millions of times larger than Earth. Each second, our sun transforms 4 million tons of mass into light, a phenomenon that is, as cosmologist Brian Swimme says, the cosmological meaning of sacrifice.[3] This gift of light is then converted by photosynthesis in plants, and we and all other life on the planet are nourished by the energy of the sun—we literally are the energy of the sun.

Ancient peoples around the world believed that the sun, the planets, and the entire universe were alive and had consciousness. During eclipses, we can observe that the sun has a corona, an aura, which has appeared to viewers as a pair of wings, a four-petaled lotus, and a four-chambered cross similar to the four-chambered cavern found deep in the heart of the Pyramid of the Sun in Teotihuacán.[4]

Biologist Rupert Sheldrake suggests that in light of the assumptions of modern science, the ancient idea that the sun and other astronomical bodies are alive may have validity. He points out that human mental activity and consciousness are associated with the complex electromagnetic patterns in our brains and that it is well established that the sun also exhibits highly complex electromagnetic patterns.[5] The complex electromagnetic patterns in the sun may well be indications of intelligence and life. Sheldrake further suggests that if the sun has a type of consciousness, the stars that make up our galaxy and the galaxies that make up the universe may also have consciousness.[6]

Most people believe that all light on this planet and resultant life comes from our sun. While there is no question that the sun gives us our physical lives, the engendering light that nourishes our consciousness comes from a central sun. This is the light that brings luminosity to our dreams and nourishes the god-seed.

Mark Griffin, the director of the Hard Light Meditation Center in Los Angeles, reminds his students that it is the Self that is the true source of consciousness. The Self, which has the illumination of a billion suns, is the central sun. Our consciousness mind is but a reflection of the light of this great omnipresent sun.

In this context, it is interesting to recall that our galaxy itself also contains a central sun, or galactic center, the point around which all the stars in our galaxy appear to revolve. It is about 23 light years away from us but invisible because it is hidden by layers of cosmic dust. There is no agreement among scientists on what this galactic center is, although it is estimated by some to be 20 million times as luminous as our sun. All galaxies seem to have central objects, and while some scientists believe they are massive black holes, others think they are central mother suns that continuously create matter and energy.[7] It is astonishing that the Maya were able to pinpoint the galactic center with such accuracy. They knew it as their place of creation and spiritual rebirth.

In spite of all our scientific sophistication, we know very little about the universe in which we live, and it seems the more we discover about the external universe, the greater the mystery. While we may never understand the nature of the metaphoric central sun, the source of all consciousness, one thing seems to be certain. We must reexamine who we are. It is unlikely we will find the inner light or the central sun from which it comes by looking outside ourselves. Nor will exploratory expeditions to Lake Titicaca find the submerged golden disk.

We need to radically shift our vision of ourselves. We come from a legacy of light. Our presence here under the reflective light of a small, yellow sun is not due to some random event that occurred eons ago in the primordial chemical soup at the edge of one of the planet's oceans. We are the result of an intentional act of creation. Some force brought light into form. We are told that we were created "into the image and similitude of God." As we are learning, evolution is an ongoing process, and we are just now realizing our godhood.

The luminous beings we know as the Elohim were our forefathers—god-like ones who planted the seed of the spiritual human deep within our forms. Their luminosity and their god-like powers are encoded in our DNA, and thus we are the seed of the great creative angels.

Divine Engendering As the Missing Evolutionary Link

There is a profound mystery regarding the stages of human development, which seem to have occurred in a series of leaps that cannot be accounted for in terms of gradual progression through time. We know that unexplained major leaps occurred approximately 50,000 to 35,000 years ago in the evolution of human consciousness—leaps that coincide with the legendary early Lemurian and Atlantian civilizations of prehistory and myth. It was around this time that evidence of human consciousness began to appear, dramatically demonstrated by the amazing artwork found in the Lascaux caverns in France, believed to be the work of Cro-Magnon man.

Life has been evolving on this planet for billions of years. Our allegedly ancestral apes appeared some 25 million years ago. Then 2 million years ago, the ape-like, man-like biped, Australopithecus appeared in Africa. Some 900,000 years later Neanderthal man appeared, who was only marginally distinguishable from his predecessors despite the long period of time that had lapsed.[8] Although he did have a significantly larger cranial capacity and was able to fashion rudimentary tools, there is no evidence he had language or a developed consciousness. Then, remarkably, a mere 50,000 to 35,000 years ago, our evolutionary process made an unprecedented leap when Homo sapiens sapiens, Cro-Magnon man, suddenly appeared. Cro-Magnon man looked and acted like us, built houses, buried his dead, and had language, art, and religion. As author Zecharia Sitchin dramatically points out in *The Twelfth Planet*, evolutionary theory cannot account for this revolutionary development, which should have taken millions of years longer. He suggests that Homo sapiens sapiens could not have been part of the same evolutionary process that led so incrementally to Neanderthal man.[9] While this missing link in human evolution has never been found by archaeologists, we do know that somehow, and quite suddenly, a series of unprecedented leaps occurred, resulting in Homo sapiens sapiens.

Sheldrake points out that myths from around the world talk about the creative tools and powers given to humans by god-men, divine heroes, and spirit beings,[10] including fire, dance, song, and language. Sheldrake states that because the stories of gifts given by spiritual beings are so universal they suggest that the evolution of human consciousness, which appears to have occurred in a series of creative leaps, may have been catalyzed by contacts with higher forms of intelligence.[11] Further, it is also instructive to note that well-documented mythic sources from around the world mentioned by Sheldrake and other scholars—including myths from cultures as diverse as the Dogon of Mali, the East Indians, and the Sumerians—point in the direction of outside intervention.[12] Even the Bible makes cryptic references to "the sons of God who consorted with the daughters of men" (Genesis 6:4). The deficiency in our evolutionary theory coupled with the rich mythic record suggest not only that there may have been outside intervention in our evolution but that outside intervention may be the only plausible explanation.

Even the most highly regarded of Christian mystics, Hildegard of Bingen, seems to have believed that the human race was engendered by the light. Hildegard of Bingen, who lived from A.D. 1098 to 1179, was the abbess of a Benedictine abbey in Germany and a great mystic, prophet, author, church reformer, and angelologist. She referred to human beings as the tenth angelic hierarchy or the tenth chorus of angels[13] and stated that God gave humans communion with the higher angelic realms,[14] an event that uniquely endowed them with higher intelligence and higher radiance.

This is not to suggest that the "communion" involved interbreeding, although some researchers suggest such literal possibilities. Contemporary angelologist Malcom Godwin amusingly points out that the mythic record indicates that angels have a certain flaw, a susceptibility to pleasures of the flesh,[15] while controversial author Erich Von Däniken surmises that our rapid human development resulted from crossbreeding with extraterrestrials or some type of genetic mutation induced by them, boldly stating that the massive Human Genome Project will someday verify whether all our genetic material was derived from our ape-like "ancestors."[16] However, such literalism may be missing the point. Angels, after all, have generally been thought of as ethereal beings who exist in subtle not physical bodies.

Myths have been described by historian William Irwin Thompson as legends of translations of experience from other dimensions into the imagery of this world.[17] The mythic records alluded to by Sheldrake and others may document actual experiences from outside of this space/time that may have dramatically transformed the blueprint of human consciousness.

Thus, it is not unreasonable to suggest that in the recent evolutionary past early humanity had "contact" with higher intelligence that resulted in a rapid and revolutionary transformation of the human form. This contact may have been interdimensional and purely energetic. Perhaps highly refined energy fields in some manner overlapped with ours, revolutionizing the human archetype. It is possible that, as esoteric teachings tell us, the seeds of the new spiritual human were planted deep within us at that time.

The Elohim, the great and mighty creative angels known as the sons of God, may well be our spiritual forebears. Although we may only have a dim subconscious memory of this contact with higher light, the Elohim may be the missing link in our evolution. If so, we are children of light who came from the angel light itself and thus have the blueprint of the angel light within us.

Accessing the Angel Light

Don Miguel Ruiz considers the angel light the stage of perception beyond the second attention. To perceive the angel light, it is necessary to make a perceptual shift. *The Physics of Angels*, a collaborative dialogue between theologian Matthew Fox and Rupert Sheldrake, shows that the angel light is not just a fluffy New Age concept. In their book they review the writings of great Christian mystics like St. Thomas Aquinas and Hildegard of Bingen on the topic of angels, in light of the discoveries of modern physics and cosmology. Angel light may actually have a basis in quantum physics. As Fox and Sheldrake point out, although many people think of angels as invisible helpers, few of us have thought of them as quantum beings.

And yet angels have features in common with aspects of quantum physics. Photons are units of light that have no mass. In the traditional literature, angels are often depicted as light-beings who have no mass.

Sheldrake points out that, like photons, angels can only be depicted by their action.[18]

Sheldrake believes that invisible fields called morphic fields determine the organization of all systems in nature—with each planet, solar system, and galaxy having its own morphic field.[19] According to this theory, the field of our planet is hierarchically included in the field of our solar system and our galaxy. Within the morphic fields are other fields such as gravitational fields and magnetic fields, as well as quantum matter fields, all of which are hierarchically nested—fields within fields.

Many ancient cultures believed that everything had a soul. Sheldrake points out that we used to think of the invisible organizing principles of nature as souls. What used to be called the soul of the universe, the *anima mundi*, we now refer to as the gravitational field. The magnetic soul is now the magnetic field; the animal soul is now the field of instinct; and the realm of mental activity is now the mental field.[20] Sheldrake suggests that angels may be an aspect of what he calls angel fields. Just as a photon is energy in the form of light that is carried by an electromagnetic field, angels may be a special energy in the form of light carried by an angel field. Like quantum particles, angels may have dual characteristics. They may be particle-like when they manifest in activity, but wave-like when they are dispersed within the field. Matthew Fox points out that when we are talking about the photon, the particle of light, and the field coming together we are describing the angel light.[21]

Further, Fox and Sheldrake explain that prior to the seventeenth-century, people believed that the universe was alive, and angels were an accepted part of their cosmology. Angels were essentially banished from Western thought by the Newtonian-Cartesian worldview. Since for the vast majority of people, angels could not be perceived with the five senses, they simply did not exist. Now due to advances in science we are beginning to free ourselves from the mechanistic view of the universe that has for so long limited our understanding, and we are beginning to understand the human quantum potential.

Traditionally, angels have been considered messengers. Fields also work as messengers. Quantum fields, gravitational fields, and electromagnetic fields all interconnect with other fields.[22] Fields are not made of matter; rather matter may be understood as energy bound within fields. Sheldrake explains that, although vibratory patterns of the electrons, protons, and neutrons exist in atomic fields, over 99 percent of such fields are empty.[23]

The essential point is that all of nature is organized by fields. The field that we may think of as the angel light is associated with consciousness and intelligence. It is this light that bridges divine light and matter. In this context, Juan Nuñez del Prado's suggestion that the light of the Pleiades acts like a joiner of energy fields, a *taqe*, is of interest. Perhaps the angel light acts as a special *taqe* in the spiritual human.

Divine light, light from which consciousness arises, is not the light that comes from our sun. Instead, it is the invisible light that we think of as inner light, the light of the Self. Our creation stories tell us that the first creation of the godhead was light. It is worth noting that our creation stories are not dissimilar to the Big Bang Theory, according to which a big bang produced a huge blaze of light, filling the entire universe. We know that we can only see a small portion of the entire light spectrum with our eyes, and thus cannot see, for example, radio waves or microwaves. It is feasible that angels are like photons, transmitting all kinds of light radiation, much of which is invisible to us.

At some point early in the development of the universe, matter separated from light. Scientifically stated, as the universe expanded and cooled there was an uncoupling of matter and radiation. Prior to that time darkness and light were undifferentiated.[24] The first light created may have been an invisible illumination, or the light of consciousness, or the angel light.

If we look at angels in the context of recent scientific discoveries, we begin to come closer to understanding the truth of both their existence and purpose. Hildegard of Bingen, whose works were based largely on mystical awareness, wrote of angels as living light,[25] as the invisible illumination that clings to living, flying spheres,[26] and stated that angels were created to function as living mirrors of divine light.

Like angels, we, too, mirror the divine when we resonate with the divine. Divine mirroring sounds remarkably similar to the Andean concept of *ayni*, or reciprocity. Thus it is likely that divine mirroring and sympathetic resonance are not only found in the angelic realms but, as the ancients of Mesoamerica and Peru believed, are part of human expression.

Most classical angelologists believed there were nine hierarchies of angels. These spheres, which we can now think of as angelic fields, order all of consciousness and span from the microcosm of human existence to the macrocosm of galactic interaction. Today, we may think of these angelic hierarchies as concentric circles of interacting light. The light within these fields not only orders and interacts with consciousness, it communicates. Like photons, angels have no mass and are not limited to the laws of the physical universe. They are, therefore, capable of communicating at super-luminal speeds. As Hildegard of Bingen clearly foresaw nearly a thousand years ago, spiritual humans are the tenth angelic hierarchy.

Gifts of the Angel Light

Finding the angel light within can be an arduous process, since to do so we must let go of many limiting beliefs and entirely re-envision ourselves. But we are not without resources. The great brotherhoods of light stand ready to assist their emergent god-seeds.

In religious literature worldwide there are many references to the elevation of perfected humans to the angelic realm.[27] Consider, for example, the familiar biblical story of Jacob. Jacob "wrestled with an angel," which has been interpreted to mean that in his quest for completion, Jacob reached the Gabriel of his own being.[28] That is, he found within himself the angel light, his true destiny.

As don Miguel Ruiz tells us, to reach the angel light we have to make a perceptual shift, since the angel light is ultimately a mystical experience. And as with all mystical experiences, after we have been engendered by the light we have to come down from the mountain. When we return from a mystical experience, we find that remarkably our world has also been transformed. We see the world differently because we are different. Because we have touched the angel light, we have within us holistic vision and the other gifts of the angel light.

Through our own striving, we will all eventually reach the angel light—it is our destiny. With the birth of the sixth sun, the spiritual human, the god-seed, is unfolding from the higher order. We have within us the radiance of the golden disk; we, too, are capable of becoming fully conscious.

Once we acknowledge ourselves as children of light we can receive the benefits that come with this legacy. The first gift of the angel light is holistic vision, the ability to see ourselves as god-seeds within an interactive galactic whole. This allows us to see who we really are and that we are all part of the light of pure consciousness. Holistic vision brings a radical shift in perspective, not only causing us to alter self-centered and destructive patterns of behavior but also to change our thinking. In addition, holistic vision allows us to understand our inherent multi-dimensionality, enabling us to access multiple aspects of our consciousness.

In this space/time, humans have physicality, but we are more than that. We are each a part of the angel light that makes up human consciousness. And by the power of our intent, we can expand upward through the nested orders of angel light to embrace the refined light of our celestial forebears. We can do this through light that connects our consciousness to the greater whole. Like the subatomic particles that define our physical structure, we are particle-like as we participate in everyday life and wavelike as our consciousness dances in unbroken wholeness. In time it is possible to make such perceptual shifts more fluidly. Through the development of our witness consciousness (a state of detached self observation, free of judgment), we can observe ourselves shifting from one state to another and perceive our simultaneous existences as the quantum beings we truly are.

Because of our multiplicity, we can consciously move between different realms of existence. We are a particle of consciousness fixed in this space/time but also a unity of consciousness beyond time or space. The gift we receive from our multiple levels of perception is that as quantum beings we can finally understand that separation is an illusion. We can begin to perceive that we are part of an ever-expanding whole and that the entire universe may itself be an immeasurable hologram that some call God.

Another gift of the angel light is unconditional love. Our new holistic vision makes it clear that we exist in an unbroken wholeness that is filled with dynamic energy and is infused with intent. The intent that pervades the angel light carries one message—unconditional love. The unifying force that pulses from the formless into form, the force that rides the waves of pure light, is the force of unconditional love. Unconditional love is the vibration that comes from the central sun, the Self. It is the superluminal force that awakens the light codes hidden in the human form, which engender the human seed, creating the capacity for divine radiance.

Unconditional love is an impersonal force that will not sustain any egotistical, false sense of Self; it only sustains the light. In contrast, personal love can at times be a beautiful and captivating illusion that can help us recognize our attachments. It is only a dream.

Unconditional love is the intent that filters from the heart of the creator and lights the hearts of the masters. It is the unifying force eternally dedicated to our awakening that filters down to this planet of a little yellow sun spinning through space in the distant realms at the far edge of the Milky Way.

Once you grasp the nature of unconditional love you realize that there is a galactic agenda. There is a higher order of complexity that is unfolding within human consciousness as a whole. Then you receive the next gift of the angel light—humility, perhaps the hardest gift to accept. After all, we learn to function within the planetary dream because we have an ego, and the better we function, the higher our self-importance. But in the angel light, there is no room for self-importance—it is, in fact, a major obstacle. Instead, it is necessary to surrender all our false pride.

Humility ultimately teaches us that all life is sacred—a gift of the divine union of form and the formless. The ancients of Wayu's time understood that everything on the planet is sacred, including every blade of grass, flower, clump of dirt, and brick. This is the critical message of the Andean masters, who perceive all objects as animate because they comprehend that everything has consciousness and acts as a receptacle of light.

When we become distracted, we slip again into perceiving things as separate, momentarily forgetting our quantum, multi-dimensional nature and losing the sacred worldview. Then as our perception shifts, we again awaken, realizing that we were seeing life from a distorted perspective. This process of reawakening is humbling and evokes deep gratitude.

The gift of gratitude leads ultimately to the practice of *ayni*. We can walk in perfect *ayni* in all worlds as the ancient ones did. As don Morales says, we can learn to perceive, think, act, and speak from a state of awareness of the sacred nature of all things. Then the world will mirror to us our sacredness. The ancient peoples of Peru and Mesoamerica knew all about the concepts of divine mirroring and sympathetic resonance. They based their cultures on these sacred principles. That is why the rare conjunction with the galactic center, the Mother Sun, may signify an extraordinary opportunity for human transformation. It is all about *ayni*.

When we practice *ayni* we have stepped into the angel light. Then the light from our golden disc shines brightly, our radiance dances superluminously through the ancient gateways of divinity, and we become quantum fields that dance in and out of form.

The Incan and Mayan prophecies point to a collective awakening of humanity, to revolutionary perceptual breakthroughs, and to stepping outside of time as we know it. They hint at a golden age of enlightenment that may represent a true quantum leap—that is, a leap to quantum consciousness, to another way of being and perceiving. We have barely entered the angel light and have yet to discover the wealth of our quantum potential.

Children of light are quantum beings who are here to walk in perfect *ayni*. We are god-seeds resonating sympathetically with the greater whole. We are fields within fields of angel light that bridge human consciousness to the higher order. *We* are the *chakarunas*, the bridge people that Wayu foresaw so long ago, and we have come to bring the full potential of divine light into human consciousness.

Glossary of Quechua and Andean Words ✵

The spelling of Quechua and Andean words used throughout this book has in many cases been adapted to facilitate their pronunciation in English.

amaru. Snake-like living energy.

apu. The spirit of a mountain, a star, or other natural feature.

ayni. To walk in balance in all three worlds of Andean reality. Based on the idea of divine reciprocity. Similar to the Christian concept of existing in a state of grace.

capacocha. The sacrificial rite held on the summer solstice. This rite was initiated by the ninth Inca, Pachacuti, and involved the sacrifice of a child from each lineage.

Capac Rayni. One of the major Incan festivals of the year. It was held on December 22, the summer solstice.

chakarunas. The bridge people.

cholla. A sacred drink made of fermented corn.

collca. Granary; a name for the Pleiades star cluster.

coto. A handful of seeds; another name for the Pleiades.

cuti. To turn upside down or to set right.

gawag. The third eye.

goya. The female counterpart of the Incan ruler, or Sapa Inca.

hanaqpacha. The superior world. This is the third level of Andean reality and it is represented by the condor. It is the home of the higher energies and supernatural spirits.

hauca. A holy or sacred place.

huanque. A double or brother.

Inca (actually inka). The illuminated one(s). This term was generally reserved for royalty.

intihuatana. A large stone used for calendric functions utilizing shadows cast by the sun.

kausay pacha. The energy universe.

kuraq. A great visionary.

kaypacha. The second level of Andean reality symbolized by the puma. The ordinary world that we perceive with the five senses.

llankay. The power associated with the physical; the ability to manifest. The body-centered person.

malku. A man who has reached the fifth level of consciousness.

mallqui. A tree; an ancestor.

mamacona. The legendary Virgins of the Sun, the select women who were specially trained in the ancient arts and who were dedicated to the service of the *pachamama*.

mastay. A great gathering of people or reintegration.

Mayu. The Milky Way, our galaxy. Also known as the sacred cosmic river.

mesayog. One who works with supernatural spirits.

mosoq karpay. A special ceremony in which, through an energetic transmission, the seed of transformation is given.

munay. The power associated with the soul, love, and feeling. The heart-centered person.

nusta. A woman who has reached the fifth level of consciousness.

Pacaritanpu. The place of emergence.

pacha. The mother or the cosmos.

pachacuti. A time of great physical or psychological transformation. Also the name of the ninth Inca.

pachamama. The Earth and all of physical creation. The feminine aspect of deity. The great Cosmic Mother, a living being that is the source of all life.

pachamag. A name for the energy of the Cosmic Father.

pag'o. A shaman.

pampa mesayog. An expert healer who works with the earth energies.

panya. By some accounts, the ordinary reality that is based on linear time and that we perceive with the physical senses. More accurately, the right side of the Andean mystical path associated with the masculine. The ordinary or left brain.

paqarinas. Places of origin or emergence from other dimensions into this time/space, such as trees, caves, and springs.

Q'ero. According to Alberto Villodo, a long-haired one, a person of knowledge, one who has healing powers. A group of Indians believed to be the last direct descendants of the Inca.

Q'ollorit'i. The annual Festival of the Snow Star, sometimes called the Return of the Pleiades.

quipuscamayocs. The record keepers. Records were kept by the arrangement of knots tied on a cord. The record keepers had the task of remembering what each knot meant. Most of the *quipus* were destroyed at the time of the conquest.

quipus. The knotted cords by which records were kept.

sapa. The Royal Inca ruler. The term *sapa* denotes an individual who has reached the sixth level of consciousness.

taqe. The third stage of relationship. The stage noted by communion, where the energy bodies interweave; also a joiner of energy fields.

Taqe Onkay. The great interweaving; the great gathering of the tribes.

Taripay Pacha. The golden age foretold in the prophecies.

tinkuy. The first stage of relationship, the encounter, where two energy bodies make contact.

tupay. The second stage of relationship. In this stage the energy bodies size each other up and feel out the potential of the encounter. The confrontation stage.

ukhapacha. The first level of Andean reality symbolized by the serpent. Known as the underground, this world is the realm of invisible things and spirits.

uru pachacuti. The transformation of the world due to water. The Great Flood.

waka. The holy statute that held the divine power of the lineage. Each tribe or lineage had their own *waka*. They believed that the *waka* connected them to the stars from where they originated.

yachay. The power of people who have knowledge and well-developed mental abilities. The mind-centered person.

yanantin. Opposites such as male and female, light and dark, viewed together as complementary pairs.

yoge. By some accounts, the non-ordinary world that functions in sacred time or dreamtime. More accurately, the left side of the Andean mystical path associated with the feminine, the right brain, and intuition.

END NOTES ✿

Chapter 1. Keepers of the Seed

1. Loren McIntyre, *The Incredible Incas and their Timeless Land* (Washington, DC: National Geographic Society, 1975), 194.

Chapter 2. Seedings of Divine Consciousness

1. William Sullivan, *The Secret of the Incas* (New York: Three Rivers Press, 1996), 23–24.
2. Fernando E. Elorrieta Salazar and Edgar Elorrieta Salazar, *The Sacred Valley of the Incas* (Cuzco: Sociedad Pacaritanpu, 1996), 24.
3. Ibid., 40.
4. See Note 1, 33; Adrian Gilbert and Maurice M. Cotterell, *The Mayan Prophecies* (Rockport, MA: Element, 1996), 139, 158.
5. David Freidel, Linda Schele, and Joy Parker, *Maya Cosmos* (New York: Quill William Morrow, 1993), 96.
6. See Note 1, 33–34.
7. See Note 1, 33.
8. See Note 1, 35; See Note 1, 371, notes 30–31.
9. J. J. Hurtak, *The Keys of Enoch* (Los Gatos, CA: The Academy of Future Science, 1977), 54.
10. Ibid., 54.
11. Peter Tompkins, *Mysteries of the Mexican Pyramids* (New York: Harper and Row, 1976), 398–401; Zecharia Stichin, *The 12th Planet* (New York: Avon Books, 1976), 336–362; Paul Von Ward, *Solarian Legacy* (Livermore, CA: Oughten House Publications, 1998), 102, 112–113; William Irwin Thompson, *The Time Falling Bodies Take to Light* (New York: St Martins Press, 1981), 28–30.
12. See Note 9, 53–54, 56.
13. See Note 9, 27–28, 54–56; See Note 11, Stichin, 336–339.
14. See Note 9, 27–28, 53–54, Manly B. Hall, *An Encyclopedic Outline of Masonic, Hermetic, Qabbalistic and Rosicrucian Symbolism* (Los Angeles: The Philosophical Research Society, 1988) LXXIII–LXXVI, CXXVI–CXXVII; See Note 11, Thompson, 25–34.
15. See Note 9, 54.
16. Malcolm Godwin, *Angels—An Endangered Species* (New York: Simon and Schuster, 1990), 177, 215–217.
17. Ibid., 214.
18. Ibid., 25.

19. Ibid., 36.

20. Ibid., 215.

21. Genesis 1: 26–27.

22. See Note 9, 27–28, 33–56.

23. See Note 9, 44.

24. Edgar Evans Cayce, Gail Cayce Schwartzer, and Douglas G. Richards, *The Mysteries of Atlantis Revisited* (New York: St. Martins Press, 1997), 1–18; See Note 11, Tompkins, 382.

25. See Note 11, Tompkins, 375–6.

26. W. Scott–Elliot, *Legends of Atlantis and Lost Lemuria* (Wheaton, IL: Quest Books, 1990) preface, xviii.

27. Ibid.

28. Timothy B. Roberts, *Gods of the Maya, Aztec, and Inca* (New York: Michael Friedman Publishing Group, 1996), 12–13.

29. See Note 11, Tompkins, 347.

30. See Note 4, Gilbert and Cotterell, 124–7; See Note 11, Tompkins, 82–83, 398–400; See Note 5, 59, 140, 196; See Note 14, Hall, CXCIII–CXCVI.

31. See Note 11, Tompkins, 399.

32. Encyclopaedia Britannica, CD, 1999, s.v. "chakra".

33. See Note 11, Thompson, 339–340.

34. See Note 11, Sitchin, 371.

35. See Note 11, Tompkins, 348–349.

36. Ibid., 166.

37. Ibid., 166.

38. Ibid., 362.

39. See Note 9, 42–46, 306, 310–312, 488; C.W. Leadbeater, *Ancient Mystic Rites* (Wheaton, IL: Quest Books, 1986), 16.

40. See Note 9, 553.

41. Corrinne Heline, *New Age Bible Interpretations: Old Testament Vol.1* (Santa Monica, CA: New Age Bible and Philosophy Center, 1938), 181.

42. Ibid., 181.

43. Ibid., 181–2.

44. See Note 39, Leadbeater, 18.

45. See Note 39, Leadbeater, 18–19, quoting from *Man; Whence, How and Whither*, 284–7.

46. See Note 11, Tompkins, 384–385, 388–389.

47. Nigel Davies, *The Toltecs Until the Fall of Tula* (Norman, OK: University of Oklahoma Press, 1977), 45.

48. See Note 11, Tompkins, 229.

49. See Note 11, Tompkins, 247.

50. Michael Rowan-Robinson, *Our Universe—An Armchair Guide* (New York: W. H. Freeman and Company, 1990), 104.

51. See Note 11, Tompkins, 266–269.

52. See Note 11, Tompkins, 263.

53. See Note 11, Tompkins, 263.

54. See Note 11, Tompkins, 263.

55. A. Yusef Ali, trans., *The Holy Qur'an* (Brentwood, MD: Amana, 1983), 907–8.

Chapter 3. Mayan and Incan Seedbeds

1. William Sullivan, *The Secret of the Incas* (New York: Three Rivers Press, 1996), 26.

2. Ibid., quoted at 27.

3. José Argüelles, *The Mayan Factor* (Santa Fe: Bear and Co., 1987), 113–118.

4. David Freidel, Linda Schele, and Joy Parker, *Maya Cosmos* (New York: Quill William Morrow, 1993), 79.

5. Ibid., 72 and 87, 85 and 87, 89–94, 76–78, respectively.

6. Ibid., 196.

7. Ibid., 92.

8. Ibid., 96.

9. Ibid., 135.

10. Ibid., 143.

11. Ibid., 139, 280.

12. Ibid., 431.

13. Ibid., 103.

14. See Note 3, 77.

15. See Note 3, 78, Peter Tompkins, *The Mysteries of the Mexican Pyramids*, (New York: Harper Row, 1976), 78–79.

16. See Note 3, 78.

17. See Note 3, 79, 52.

18. See Note 3, 79.

19. See Note 1, 7.

20. John Major Jenkins, *Maya Cosmogenesis 2012* (Santa Fe: Bear and Co., 1998), xxxvii.

21. Ibid., xxxviii.

22. Ibid., 106.

23. Ibid., 111.

24. Ibid., 113–4.

25. Ibid., 91–102.

26. J. J. Hurtak, *The Keys of Enoch* (Los Gatos, CA: The Academy of Future Science, 1977), 78.

27. See Note 3, 174.

28. Alice Howell, *Jungian Synchronicity in Astrological Signs and Ages* (Wheaton, IL: Quest Books, 1990), 20.

29. Michael Talbolt, *Holographic Universe*, (New York: Harper Perennial, 1991), 290.

30. Fernando E. Elorrieta Salazar and Edgar Elorrieta Salazar, *The Sacred Valley of the Incas—Myths and Symbols* (Cuzco: Sociedad Pacaritanpu Hatha, 1996), 101.

31. See Note 1, 204–7.

32. See Note 1, 214.

33. See Note 1, 208.

34. See Note 1, 208.

35. See Note 1, 207–11.

36. See Note 1, 303.

37. Loren Mc Intyre, *The Incredible Incas and Their Timeless Land* (Washington, DC: National Geographic Society, 1975), 31.

38. See Note 1, 29.

39. See Note 1, 262.

40. Timothy B. Roberts, *The Gods of the Maya, Aztecs and Inca* (New York: Michael Friedman Publishing Group, 1996), 75.

41. See Note 1, 312.

42. See Note 1, 313.

43. See Note 1, 324.

44. See Note 1, 257, Frank Waters, *Mexican Mystique* (Athens, OH: Swallow Press, 1975), 123.

45. See Note 1, 256.

46. See Note 1, 279.

47. See Note 1, 333.

48. See Note 1, 341.

49. See Note 34, 9.

50. See Note 1, 390; See Note 40, 74.

Chapter 4. Andean Prophecies of a New Age

1. Alberto Villoldo, "Inca Prophecies of the End of Time," *Four Winds Society* 1995–1996. Also personal correspondance between the author and Joan Parisi Wilcox.

2. See Note 1, Villoldo, Elizabeth Jenkins, *Initiation—A Woman's Spiritual Journey* (New York: G. P. Putnam and Sons, 1997), 234, 235.

3. See Note 2, Jenkins, 227-228, 230.

4. Hal Zina Bennett, "From the Heart of the Andes: An Interview with Q'ero Incan Shamans," *Shaman's Drum*, Issue 36, Fall 1994, 36, 40–49.

5. Joan Parisi Wilcox, *Keepers of the Ancient Knowledge* (Boston: Element, 1999), 180–181.

6. Joan Parisi Wilcox, "Stepping Outside of Time—Q'ero Shamanism and the West," *Magical Blend*, Issue 44, November, 1994, 45–48, 84–86.

7. Ibid.

8. See Note 4.

9. Alberto Villoldo and Erik Jendresen, *The Island of the Sun* (Rochester, NY: Destiny Books, 1992), 175.

10. Sound recording, "The End," John Lennon and Paul McCartney, *Abbey Road*, (Northern Songs, 1969).

11. See Note 9, 175.

12. See Note 4.

13. See Note 1, Villoldo, 2.

14. See Note 1, Villoldo, 2.

15. See Note 1, Villoldo, 2.

16. Brad Berg, "Prophecies of the Q'ero Incan Shamans," *Share International Magazine*, January/February, 1997.

17. J. L. Gferer, "Four Steps to Power and Knowledge," *Four Winds Society, 1995–1996.*

18. See Note 2, Jenkins, 229, 236.

19. See Note 2, Jenkins, 229.

20. Personal conversations between the author and don Miguel Ruiz.

21. See Note 5, 243–245.

22. William Sullivan, *The Secret of the Incas* (New York: Three Rivers Press, 1996), 37, 51, 55.

23. See Note 2, Jenkins, 263-5.

24. See Note 2, Jenkins, 264-5.

Chapter 5. Awakening

1. Frank Waters, *The Mexican Mystique* (Athens, OH: Swallow Press, 1975), 246.
2. Ibid., Sklower appendix, 285–304.
3. Ibid., 282.
4. C. G. Jung, *Flying Saucers: A Modern Myth of things Seen in the Skies*, R.F.C. Hull, trans. (Princeton, MA: Princeton University Press, 1991), 5.
5. Mary Carroll Nelson, *Beyond Fear, a Toltec Guide to Freedom and Joy—the Teachings of Miguel Angel Ruiz M.D.*(Tulsa, OK: Council Oaks Books, 1997), 30. Also personal conversations between the author and don Miguel Ruiz.
6. Ibid., 31.
7. Matthew Fox and Rupert Sheldrake, *The Physics of Angels* (San Francisco: Harper San Francisco, 1996), 101.
8. Michael Talbot, *Holographic Universe* (New York: Harper Perennial, 1991), 123–5.
9. Richard Gerber, *Vibrational Medicine* (Santa Fe: Bear and Co., 1988), 59.
10. See Note 7, 41–43.
11. Victor Sanchez, *The Teachings of Don Carlos* (Santa Fe: Bear and Co., 1996), 23.
12. Gregg Braden, *Awakening to Zero Point* (Questa, NM: Sacred Spaces/Ancient Wisdom, 1994), 178.
13. Sidney Liebes, Elizabet Sahtouris and Brian Swimme, *A Walk Through Time* (New York: John Wiley & Sons, 1998), 27.
14. Edgar Mitchell, keynote presentation, "Nature's Mind—The Quantum Hologram," Conference on Science and Consciousness, April 11, 1999, Albuquerque, NM.
15. Gary Zukav, *The Seat of the Soul* (New York: Simon and Schuster, 1989), 106.

Chapter 6. Libraries of Antiquity

1. H. H. the Dalai Lama, *The Good Heart*, (Boston: Wisdom Publications, 1996), 121.
2. James Swan, *Sacred Places* (Santa Fe: Bear and Co., 1990), 35.
3. Peter Tompkins, *Mysteries of the Mexican Pyramids* (New York: Harper and Row, 1976), 326.
4. Ibid., 327.
5. Ibid., 330–1.
6. Ibid., 327.
7. Ibid., 328.
8. Ibid., 328.

9. Ibid., 327.

10. Ibid., 328.

11. Ibid., 326, 328–9.

12. Sid Lonegren, *Spiritual Dowsing* (Glastonbury: Gothic Image Publications, 1986), 34–35.

13. Paul Devereux, *Earth Memory* (St Paul, MN: Llewllyn, 1992), 183.

14. See Note 12, 35.

15. See Note 13, 129.

16. See Note 13, 276–7.

17. See Note 13, 274–6; See Note 2, 75–115.

18. See Note 3, 314.

19. See Note 3, 261–3.

20. Personal conversations between the author and don Miguel Ruiz.

21. Michael Talbot, *Holographic Universe* (New York: Harper Perennial, 1991), 174–6.

22. See Note 12, 302.

23. Victor Sanchez, *The Teachings of Don Carlos* (Santa Fe: Bear and Co., 1995), 8.

24. Ibid., 10.

25. Ibid.,131–6.

26. See Note 21, 163.

27. See Note 2, 86–102.

28. See Note 2, 209.

29. Elizabeth B. Jenkins, *Initiation—A Woman's Spiritual Journey* (New York: G.P. Putnam and Sons, 1997), 130.

30. José Argüelles, *The Mayan Factor* (Santa Fe: Bear and Co., 1987), 147–8.

31. Ibid., 154.

32. See Note 21, 293.

Chapter 7. Stepping Into the Angel Light

1. Manly B. Hall, *The Encyclopedic Outline of Masonic, Hermetic, Qabblistic and Rosicrucian Symbolism* (Los Angeles: The Philosophical Research Society, 1988), CXCIV.

2. Brother Phillip, *Secret of the Andes* (San Rafael, CA: Leaves of Grass Press, 1961), 13–15.

3. Brian Swimme, *The Hidden Heart of the Cosmos* (Mary Knoll, NY: Orbis Books, 1996), 39–40.

4. Frank Waters, *Mexican Mystique* (Athens, OH: Swallow Press, 1975), 205.

5. Matthew Fox and Rupert Sheldrake, *The Physics of Angels* (San Francisco: Harper San Francisco, 1996), 18.

6. Ibid., 18–20.

7. Paul A. Laviolette, *Beyond the Big Bang* (Rochester, VT: Park Street Press, 1995), 239.

8. Zecharia Sitchin, *The 12th Planet* (New York: Avon Books, 1978), 17.

9. Ibid., 17.

10. See Note 5, 164.

11. See Note 5, 164.

12. See Note 8, 336–362, Paul Von Ward, *Solarian Legacy* (Livermore, CA: Oughten House Publications, 1998), 102, 112–113; Peter Tompkins, *Mysteries of the Mexican Pyramids* (New York: Harper and Row, 1976), 398–399; William Irwin Thompson, *The Time Falling Bodies Take to Light* (New York: St Martins Press, 1981), 28–30; Richard Laurence, trans., *The Book of Enoch, the Prophet* (San Diego, CA: Secret Doctrine Reference Series, Wizards Bookshelf, 1995), 5–7.

13. See Note 5, 161.

14. Ibid., 162.

15. Malcolm Godwin, *Angels—An Endangered Species* (New York: Simon and Schuster, 1990), 69–72.

16. Erich Von Daniken, *The Return of the Gods* (Shaftesbury, Dorset: Element, 1995), 138.

17. See Note 12, Thompson, 39.

18. See Note 5, 21.

19. See Note 5, 39.

20. See Note 5, 39–40.

21. See Note 5, 41.

22. See Note 5, 42.

23. See Note 5, 50.

24. See Note 5, 85.

25. See Note 5, 138.

26. See Note 5, 139.

27. See Note 5, Manly B. Hall, *An Encyclopedic Outline of Masonic, Hermetic, Qabbalistic and Rosicrucian Symbolism* (Los Angeles: The Philosophical Research Society, 1988), 139.

28. Peter Lamborn Wilson, (New York: Pantheon Press, 1980), 179.

29. Ibid., 186.

SELECTED BIBLIOGRAPHY

Argüelles, José. *The Mayan Factor.* Santa Fe: Bear and Co., 1987.

Braden, Gregg. *Awakening to Zero Point.* Questa, NM: Sacred Spaces/Ancient Wisdom, 1994.

Cayce, Edgar Evans, Gail Joyce Schwartzer, and Douglas G. Richards. *Mysteries of Atlantis Revisited.* New York: St. Martins Press, 1997.

Capra, Fritof. *The Tao of Physics.* Boston: Shambala Press, 1991.

Chopra, Deepak. *Quantum Healing.* New York: Bantam, 1992.

Castenada, Carlos. *The Teachings of Don Juan.* Berkeley: University of California Press, 1986.

———. *A Separate Reality.* Berkeley: New York: Simon and Schuster, 1971.

Devereux, Paul. *Earth Memory.* St Paul, MN: Llewellyn, 1992.

Fox, Matthew and Rupert Sheldrake. *The Physics of Angels.* San Francisco: Harper San Francisco, 1996.

Freidel, David, Linda Schele, and Joy Parker. *Maya Cosmos.* New York: Quill William Morrow, 1993.

Gerber, Richard. *Vibrational Medicine.* Santa Fe: Bear and Co., 1988.

Godwin, Malcolm. *Angels an Endangered Species.* New York: Simon and Schuster, 1990.

Goswami, Amit. *The Self Aware Universe.* San Francisco: J. P. Tarcher, 1995.

Hall, Manly B. *An Encyclopedic Outline of Masonic, Hermetic, Qabbalistic and Roscirucian Symbolism.* Los Angeles: The Philosophical Research Society, Inc., 1988.

Heline, Corinne 1993. *New Age Bible Interpretations: Old Testament, Vol. I.* Santa Monica, CA: New Age Bible and Philosophy Center, 1993.

Heselton, Philip. *Earth Mysteries.* Rockport, NY: Element, 1991.

Hunt, Valerie V. *Infinite Mind.* Malibu, CA: Malibu Publishing, 1996.

Hurtak, J. J. *The Keys of Enoch.* Los Gatos, CA: The Academy of Future Science, 1977.

Jenkins, Elizabeth B. *Initiation, A Woman's Spiritual Journey.* New York: G. P. Putnam and Sons, 1997.

Jenkins, John Major. *Maya Cosmogenesis 2012.* Santa Fe: Bear and Co., 1998.

Jung, C.G. 1959. *Flying Saucers: A Modern Myth of Things Seen in the Sky.* Translated by R.F.C. Hull. New York: Harcourt, Brace, 1959.

Laviolette, Paul A. *Beyond the Big Bang.* Rochester, NY: Park Street Press, 1995.

Leadbeater, C.W. *Ancient Mystic Rites.* Wheaton, IL: Quest Books, 1986.

Liebes, Sidney, Elisabet Sahtouris, and Brian Swimme. *A Walk Through Time.* New York: John Wiley & Sons, 1998.

Lonegren, Sig. *Spiritual Dowsing*. Glastonbury: Gothic Image Publications, 1986.

Michell, John 1983. *New View Over Atlantis*. London: Thames and Hudon, 1983.

Ruiz, Miguel. *The Four Agreements*. San Rafael, CA: Amber-Allen Publications, 1997.

Salazar, Fernando E. Elorrieta, and Edgar Elorrieta Salazar. *The Sacred Valley of the Incas Myths and Symbols*. Cusco: Sociedad Pacaritanpu Hatha, 1996.

Sanchez, Victor. *The Teachings of Don Carlos*. Santa Fe: Bear and Co., 1995.

Schele, Linda, and David Freidel. *Forest of Kings*. New York: William Morrow and Company, Inc., 1990.

Scott-Elliot, W. *Legends of Atlantis and Lost Lemuria*. Wheaton, IL: Quest Books, 1990.

Singh, Madanjeet, *The Sun Symbol and Power of Life*. New York: Harry N. Abrams, 1993.

Sitchin, Zecharin, *The 12th Planet*. New York: Avon Books, 1976.

Steiner, Rudolf, *Cosmic Memory: Atlantis and Lemuria*. Blauvelt: Rudolf Steiner Publications, 1971.

Sullivan, William. *The Secret of the Incas*. New York: Three Rivers Press, 1996.

Swan, James. *Sacred Places*. Santa Fe: Bear and Co, 1990.

Swimme, Brian. *The Hidden Heart of the Cosmos*. Mary Knoll, NY: Orbis Books, 1996.

Talbot, Michael. *Holographic Universe*. New York: Harper Perennial, 1991.

Tompkins, Peter. *Mysteries of the Mexican Pyramids*. New York: Harper and Row, 1976.

Thompson, Keith. *Angels and Aliens*. New York: Ballantine, 1993.

Thompson, William Irwin. *The Time Falling Bodies Take to Light*. New York: St Martins Press, 1981.

Villoldo, Alberto, and Erik Jendresen. *The Dance of the Four Winds*. Rochester, NY: Destiny Books, 1990.

———. *The Island of the Sun*. Rochester, NY: Destiny Books, 1990.

Von Daniken, Erich. *The Return of the Gods*. Shaftesbury, Dorset: Element, 1997.

Von Ward, Paul, *Solarian Legacy*. Livermore, CA: Oughten House Publications, 1998.

Waters, Frank 1963. *The Book of the Hopi*. Middlesex: Penguin, 1963.

Waters, Frank. *Mexican Mystique*. Athens, OH: Swallow Press, 1975.

Wilcox, Joan Parisi. *Keepers of the Ancient Knowledge*. Boston: Element, 1999.

Zukav, Gary. *The Dancing Wu Li Masters*. Toronto: Bantam, 1979.

———. *The Seat of the Soul*. New York: Simon and Schuster, 1989.

INDEX ✵

AUTHOR'S NOTE ❧

For information on related books, materials, and workshops, please send a self-addressed stamped envelope (foreign inquiries include an international postage coupon) to:

> Web-of-Light
> 305 E. 4th Street
> Washburn, WI 54891

Or contact our internet site at:
> www.web-of-light.com

BOOKS OF RELATED INTEREST

THE TUTANKHAMUN PROPHECIES
The Sacred Secret of the Maya, Egyptians, and Freemasons
by Maurice Cotterell

MAYA COSMOGENESIS 2012
The True Meaning of the Maya Calendar End-Date
by John Major Jenkins

THE MYSTERY OF THE CRYSTAL SKULLS
A Real Life Detective Story of the Ancient World
by Chris Morton and Ceri Louise Thomas

THE LOST REALMS
by Zecharia Sitchin

CATASTROPHOBIA
The Truth Behind Earth Changes in the Coming Age of Light
by Barbara Hand Clow

THE SECRETS OF MAYAN SCIENCE/RELIGION
by Hunbatz Men

FROM THE ASHES OF ANGELS
The Forbidden Legacy of a Fallen Race
by Andrew Collins

THE SIRIUS MYSTERY
New Scientific Evidence of Alien Contact 5,000 Years Ago
by Robert Temple

Inner Traditions • Bear & Company
P.O. Box 388
Rochester, VT 05767
1-800-246-8648
www.InnerTraditions.com

Or contact your local bookseller